SĀDHANĀ
OF THE
HEART

SIDDHA YOGA MESSAGES FOR THE YEAR
VOLUME I : 1995—1999

SĀDHANĀ OF THE HEART

A collection of talks on spiritual life
by

GURUMAYI CHIDVILĀSĀNANDA

A SIDDHA YOGA® PUBLICATION / PUBLISHED BY SYDA FOUNDATION, SOUTH FALLSBURG, NY
www.siddhayoga.org

Published by SYDA Foundation
PO Box 600, 371 Brickman Rd, South Fallsburg, NY 12779, USA

ACKNOWLEDGMENTS

Warm thanks to all of those who offered their sevā *so generously toward the publication of the first volume of* Sādhanā of the Heart: *to the editors, Kshamā Ferrar and Sarah Scott, and the editorial consultant, Kathryn Downing; to Stéphane Dehais for the cover design; to Christopher Wallis, the Sanskrit consultant; to Cynthia Briggs, Valerie Sensabaugh, and Ely White, the copyeditors; to Vladimir Klimenchenko and Crystal Henning for typesetting; to Judith Levi for the index; to Lissa Feldman for research; to Francois Simon for coordinating the print production; and to the Siddha Yoga students whose donations covered the cost of publishing the first volume of* Sādhanā of the Heart.

Pamela Williams, Managing Editor
SYDA Publications

Printed in the United States of America
First published 2006

16 15 14 13 12 11 2 3 4 5 6

Library of Congress Cataloging-in-Publication Data.

Chidvilasananda, Gurumayi.
Sadhana of the heart : a collection of talks on spiritual life / by Gurumayi Chidvilasananda.
v. cm.
"A Siddha Yoga publication."
Includes bibliographical references and index.
Contents: v. 1. Siddha yoga messages for the year, 1995-1999.
ISBN 1-930939-05-1 (v. 1)
1. Siddha yoga (Service mark) 2. Spiritual life. I. Title.
BL1283.792.C45A277 2006
294.5'44--dc22

2006012834

ABOUT THE SYDA FOUNDATION

The SYDA Foundation is a not-for-profit organization that protects, preserves, and disseminates the Siddha Yoga teachings of Gurumayi Chidvilāsānanda, Swāmī Muktānanda, and Bhagavān Nityānanda. The SYDA Foundation also guides the philanthropic expressions of the Siddha Yoga path. These include The PRASAD Project, which provides health, education, and sustainable development programs for children, families, and communities in need; and the Muktabodha Indological Research Institute, which helps to preserve the scriptural heritage of India.

NOTE ON THE TEXT

All of the Siddha Yoga Message talks in *Sādhanā of the Heart* were produced as audio and visual recordings; some of these talks are also included in published collections of Gurumayi's teachings. (See Further Reading, pages 155-158.) Minor differences that occur between audio/visual versions and the written text reflect stylistic differences between the spoken and the printed word.

Throughout the text, the standard international transliteration conventions for South Asian languages have been employed. Sanskrit and Hindi terms appear in the text in italics; proper names are printed in roman type. For the reader's convenience, a Sanskrit pronunciation guide is included on pages 126-127.

CONTENTS

FOREWORD

Sādhanā of the Heart, a collection of talks by Gurumayi Chidvilāsānanda, is a modern scripture, shining with the power of Gurumayi's enlightened state and her loving intention for the spiritual progress of every human being. Each of the talks in *Sādhanā of the Heart* was originally presented to Siddha Yoga students as a message for the new year,[1] and each one endures as a focus of contemplation and a source of revelation.

Gurumayi Chidvilāsānanda is a Siddha Guru, a Master who has achieved the highest attainment of the spiritual path. Established permanently in the full awareness of universal divinity — that supreme perfection inherent in everything and everyone in the universe — Gurumayi is able to guide others to this same awareness.

For thirty-five years I have been a student of the Gurus of the Siddha Yoga path: first of Swāmī Muktānanda, Gurumayi's Guru, and then, after his passing in 1982, of Gurumayi Chidvilāsānanda. In the more than two decades of studying with Gurumayi, I have experienced, and have seen many others experience, the depth of caring from which her teachings spring. *Sādhanā of the Heart* is an example of her compassion. Every talk in this collection is illumined by Gurumayi's enlightened experience; every talk brims with philosophical knowledge and practical guidance for reaching the liberated state that she herself attained by following the Siddha Yoga path. Gurumayi shares with us the experience and wisdom of her own *sādhanā.* Her message is clear and strong: this state is possible for you. You can, with commitment, strong intention, and focused effort, live in the fullness of your own divinity, and you can share it with others. You can truly live in freedom and love.

Woven through all of these Message talks is a common thread concerning spiritual practice. As Gurumayi says, "Basically, every one of . . . [these Messages] emphasizes the purification of the heart."[2]

The heart — *hṛdaya* in Sanskrit — is a central theme in all of Gurumayi's teachings. In traditional Sanskrit literature, *hṛdaya* stands for the core, for what is essential. Many subtleties of meaning are conveyed by this one term; some of them refer to the individual and some refer to the supreme Self, the Consciousness that pervades the universe.

On the individual level, the most obvious meaning refers to the physical heart, which for thousands of years has served poets and sages as a metaphor for other fundamental aspects of our being. In certain texts on yoga, the word *heart* connotes a spiritual center, or *cakra,* within a human being. Other texts speak about "the knot of the heart," a subtle blockage that a yogi must pierce or dissolve to attain liberation. Saints of India often speak of the heart as "the subjective principle" of an individual, the psychic instrument, which in Western culture is called the mind.

On the level of universal Consciousness, we read in the Upaniṣads about "the cave of the Heart," the abode of the great light of Consciousness in the subtle body. Some Shaivite texts of Kashmir use the term *Heart* to refer to the supreme Self, which pervades each of us and everything in creation.

In the Siddha Yoga Message talks, Gurumayi uses the term *heart* in both of these senses.* In some instances she speaks of the heart as the center of our feelings, thoughts, sensations, memories, and past impressions — as the psychic instrument within the physical body. It is this meaning of the word that Gurumayi uses when she speaks about purifying the heart. Understood in this way, the heart makes us experience ourselves as individuals with distinct characteristics and personalities. As Gurumayi explains:

> To change your attitude, to feel that everything in your life is sublime, your heart must be completely purified in the fire of grace.[3]

---

*In the text when the word *heart* refers to the individual, it is spelled with a lowercase *h*. Referring to universal Consciousness, *Heart* is spelled with an uppercase *H*. In some passages, you may discover that the word can be understood in both senses. When you notice this, you can explore for yourself the play between the two meanings of the word.

Gurumayi also speaks about the Heart as our essential Self, the light of divinity within all of creation. In this sense, the Heart is stainless, eternal, and ever blissful. To become established in this higher Self is the sole purpose of *sādhanā*, spiritual practice. In her 1995 Message talk, Gurumayi says:

> When you perceive the light of your own Heart permeating the entire universe, you have the amazing experience of oneness. The mind is so astonished by this divine splendor that all it wants to do is lower its head in awe and follow the command of the Lord. The experience never leaves you. Everywhere you go, it is with you.[4]

The journey of the spirit is the purification of our individual heart so that we may fully experience the effulgent Heart, the pulsating center of all that exists. This is the essence of the *sādhanā* that Gurumayi inspires each one of us to undertake.

To be a student of Siddha Yoga involves a gradual, step-by-step assimilation and application of the teachings given by the Gurus of the Siddha Yoga path. The initial step is to apprehend and consider carefully the instructions given by the Master, who has walked the path and who lives in the enlightened experience of its unwavering attainment. A seeker, eager to experience the goal of yoga, participates consciously in this classical transmission of wisdom: the Guru imparts the knowledge and we, as fully alert students, engage with it. Once we have understood the import of the Guru's teachings, the crucial next step is to begin to incorporate these teachings actively into our day-to-day life. As we move forward on the inner journey, we continually practice this sequence of hearing, contemplating, and applying the Guru's teachings; steadily we refine our understanding, coming ever closer to the permanent experience of the Heart.

By persevering devotedly in yoga, we allow the deepest Truth, the wisdom of the supreme Power in every human being, to shine through us. As we follow the spiritual path with commitment, taking responsibility for our own forward motion, a gradual renewal occurs whereby we become embodiments of the teachings to which our study, practices, and actions are dedicated.

For the Guru's teachings to dwell fully in our mind and shine in all their integrity through our actions, our perception of our essential nature must be purified and expanded. This transformation happens through personal effort and the support of grace. A distinctive characteristic of the Siddha Yoga Gurus is the capacity to awaken within a seeker the power of grace, which scriptural texts of India refer to as *kuṇḍalinī śakti*. This extraordinary and most fortunate event is known as *śaktipāt dīkṣā*, literally, "initiation by descent of divine Power." The awakened power of *kuṇḍalinī* supports our efforts to move forward along the path, nourishing our spiritual endeavors and guiding us toward the light that is our true Self. Gurumayi describes this process in the Message talk of 1996:

> Siddha Yoga is the yoga of grace, the abundant grace of the Master. Freely and spontaneously this grace enters the lives of seekers. Yet for the Guru's grace to unfold in its fullness, it demands that seekers put forth a sincere effort to reach the goal of their seeking.[5]

Supported by grace, our efforts to comprehend and implement the Siddha Yoga teachings and practices bring about an inner transformation, opening the way for us to perceive the amazing light of God in ourselves and in all creation. This scintillating light is the true Heart. It is our true Self.

One of my favorite aphorisms from Gurumayi's teachings describes the relationship between grace and effort in three words: "Grace follows effort." Once a person receives initiation by *śaktipāt* from the Guru, the awakened *kuṇḍalinī śakti* performs from within the process of purification and reveals the insights that create a new sense of who we are. Ultimately, it is grace that dissolves our sense of separation from the divine Self. And yet, let us be very clear, our own effort in *sādhanā* is indispensable. This teaching stands out prominently in the Siddha Yoga Message talks. Gurumayi wishes us to grasp an inescapable truth about the spiritual journey: to attain the joy and freedom promised by the path of yoga, we have to do our own work. This work is the effort of *sādhanā*.

In the context of the Siddha Yoga teachings, *sādhanā* — "that which leads straight to a goal" — refers to the ensemble of spiritual practices given by the Siddha Guru for seekers to reach the highest attainment. These practices are meditation, chanting of the divine Name and scriptural texts, selfless service, offering of *dakṣiṇā*, study and contemplation of the Guru's teachings, and repetition of the mantra. Through these practices we develop our innate virtues, nurturing and expanding the divine Power within.

The grace of *kuṇḍalinī śakti* always accompanies our spiritual practice; it is there to deepen our meditation, it intensifies the sweetness that comes from our chanting, it sharpens the insights gained through our contemplation, it expands the generosity that comes from offering *dakṣiṇā*, and it brings out the love for others that arises from selfless service, *sevā*. However, for these fruits to ripen, our effort must be constant and strong.

What supports constancy and strength in *sādhanā*? *Sādhanā of the Heart* is unequivocal in its answer to this question. One must cultivate what Gurumayi has called "the magnificent virtues," such as equipoise, enthusiasm, courage, resolution, and love. One must live according to the Heart's consent, creating a golden mind, relishing silence, and enhancing trust. One must experience the supreme Power within. These are ways to build the nobility of character that brings us closer and closer to the Guru's state.

Each of these virtues offers an indispensable and practical approach to attaining the supreme goal. Each leads to what the sages of the nondual Shaivite philosophy of Kashmir call *pratyabhijñā* — the recognition of divinity within ourselves and the experience of that divinity in all creation.[6] The virtues extolled by Gurumayi express our true humanity and generosity, and at the same time enhance the quality of life for those with whom we come in contact.

People sometimes ask, "Isn't meditation a selfish act? How can meditation and the path of yoga contribute to the improvement of our world?" Of course, it is true that a person can meditate for hours and hours and still be nasty to the neighbors. A person can profess great devotion for God and still be arrogant and condescending. We can perform so-called service and continue to behave with selfishness. For me, such contradictions illustrate the importance of remembering this central principle of the Siddha Yoga path: we must *embody* the teachings so that they shape us thoroughly, and so that we express them naturally in our own individual style and in all the particulars of our life. As Gurumayi encourages us: become a true human being!

When we practice the virtues that Gurumayi so eloquently enunciates in *Sādhanā of the Heart,* and when we perform our spiritual practices with perseverance and dedication, we find ourselves naturally living in harmony with the people and the world around us. For this reason, Siddha Yoga *sādhanā* develops simultaneously in two directions: on the one hand, it is introspective and unfurls our inner potential; on the other hand, it is extroverted and enhances our relationship with the surrounding world. Such is the essence of divine recognition, *pratyabhijñā:* the Consciousness that is within as our inner Self is the same Consciousness that is outside as the universe.

The unfolding of the *sādhanā* of the Heart takes place within this human body — and the life of a human body is finite. A wise seeker remains aware of this reality. Gurumayi reminds us frequently of the immense value of time. At the beginning of the Message for 2001, for example, she says:

> As a seeker, it is essential for you to remember that you are on the spiritual path. It is imperative for you to know that you are seeking liberation. It is vital for you to keep in mind that you want to become the supreme Being. How are you going to reach the goal? You must harness the power of the present moment.[7]

Such statements evoke reflection: "Am I making the best use of my time? How long am I going to wait to fulfill my longing for God?" We may observe from this self-inquiry that our initial enthusiasm to attain the deepest purpose of human life has become lukewarm. It may even be that our purpose has wandered astray and is hiding in a dim corner of our memory.

Gurumayi calls upon us to consider, and reconsider, right now in this present moment, our notions about the meaning of life and our role in this world. Every moment in time is an opportunity to make a choice about how we are leading our lives. Every moment we can remind ourselves: "I am on the spiritual path; I am seeking liberation; I want to become the supreme Being." We can ask ourselves with earnest regard for the response: "How am I going to reach the goal?"

Through our study and contemplation of these Siddha Yoga Messages, we have a most rare and beneficial opportunity to immerse ourselves in the wisdom of a Siddha Master, to discover new ways to incorporate these teachings into our lives, to refine our spiritual practices, and to strengthen our resolve as we move forward in our own *sādhanā* of the Heart.

May your study of the Siddha Yoga Messages bring the freshness of new beginnings to each moment of your life!

Swāmī Shāntānanda
Shree Muktānanda Ashram
South Fallsburg, New York
October 2005

SWĀMĪ SHĀNTĀNANDA has been a student of the Siddha Yoga path since 1972 under the guidance of both Gurumayi Chidvilāsānanda and Swāmī Muktānanda. He has served as a Siddha Yoga teacher since 1974, and in 1977 he was initiated by Swāmī Muktānanda into the Sarasvatī order of monks. Swāmī Shāntānanda is the author of *The Splendor of Recognition: An Exploration of the* Pratyabhijñā-hṛdayam, *a Text on the Ancient Science of the Soul.*

BLAZE THE TRAIL OF EQUIPOISE
AND ENTER THE HEART,
THE DIVINE SPLENDOR

Siddha Yoga Message for the Year 1995

WITH GREAT RESPECT, WITH GREAT LOVE, I welcome you all with all my heart.

Infinity in a finite instant, a fraction of a second, the tiniest particle, barely a speck inside infinity: the play of Consciousness emerges and dissolves. The heart leaps up and swirls in benevolent light. Our days wash over us in shining waves. Twilight lures the tired mind. The dawn awakens the yearning for worship.

Time is immeasurable, and yet, we measure our lives by it. Time weaves a web of illusions. Time also erases illusions, memories, latent impressions. Actions are forgotten; impulses fade.

Darkness is time. The light of day is time. Time is innocent. Time is pure. Time is empty. And yet, everything happens in time.

Now at this very instant, 1995 is unfolding before our eyes. We must be with this year, every minute of it, and we must also transcend its trappings. As 1995 whirls before us, showing its fiery magic, its secret agenda, its display of promises, its bait of the fulfillment of wishes, its compassion in making all our bright resolutions come true — as all of this comes to pass, we must be vigilant. We must not hand over full responsibility for ourselves, or for our time, to the year 1995.

It is the *dharma,* the sacred duty, of each person to know that which is beyond the known, to experience that which is beyond the senses, to give oneself to the Lord of time who governs the universe.

Everyone is waiting with great exhilaration — and a little trepidation — to hear the Message for 1995 from the Siddha Yoga perspective. It is my good fortune to convey it. The Message for 1995 is *Blaze the trail of equipoise and enter the Heart, the divine splendor.*

Equipoise — a balanced state of mind. In today's age, which is called *kali-yuga,* the age of darkness, equipoise has become crucial. For centuries, all human beings have endeavored to know the Truth, the great Truth within themselves, and to stay in touch with it as they go about their daily duties. This aspiration, this great understanding, has always been considered exceptionally difficult. Grasping the Truth, living by its principles, sharing knowledge equally with your fellow beings — none of this is easy.

As Mahātmā Gandhi once said:

> It is not so difficult to endure bullets in your chest;
> but it is extremely difficult to work daily on a schedule,
> to fight with yourself at every moment, and in this way,
> to purify yourself.[1]

These were not empty words. In the thick of *kali-yuga,* Mahātmā Gandhi lived by them. As many of you know, during his last day on this earth, Gandhi was torn apart by bullets. In the shock of those final moments, as the bullets struck, what came out of his being? *"He Rām! He Rām! He Rām!"* "O Lord!" What an example he set. For years Gandhi performed spiritual practices in a disciplined way, no matter where he was or what was going on around him. He blazed a trail to equipoise, and it did not desert him in his hour of need. *"He Rām!"* he cried, for that was his mantra.

To enter the Heart and behold the divine splendor is the summit of human reality. It is the highest blessing that destiny can confer. It is the accumulation of the countless merits of one's good deeds in lifetime after lifetime.

Begin blazing this trail for yourself right now. Don't wait a moment longer. Time is so elusive, and such a trickster, too. It makes you think you have all the time in the world. Then you find that there isn't even a grain of time left for you. You don't even have a minute in which to think about what to do. So, to take hold of the time before you, to make the best out of what you have, you must gather up all your courage, patience, and concentration. You must blaze a trail through *saṁsāra,* the world of the wandering, and reach the state of equipoise.

Once again, what is equipoise? It is a state where everything is tranquil, though it is in movement; where everything moves, yet is serene. This state is definitely a hard-earned treasure. Once you have attained it, you can truly call yourself worthy to step into the Heart and drink the nectar of divine splendor.

Why do we say, "Blaze the trail of equipoise"? This is *sādhanā,* the *sādhanā* of seekers. You must blaze the trail so that you clear the way and prepare the ground, not only for yourself but also for those who will be following the same path. You must make it easier for them to tread.

What is your companion as you go? Renunciation. The state of equipoise can only be attained through the power of renunciation. First, you must become detached from all the worldly things that stand in the way of sublime perception. Then, you can have the *darśan* of your own great Self. To blaze the trail, you must be equipped with this great quality, renunciation, the unburdening of the soul.

Bābā Muktānanda often spoke about renunciation. On one occasion he said:

> Renounce not God, but renounce lack of faith in God. Renounce instability and laziness. You should be able to pick out all of the tendencies of your mind that operate against devotion to God, and uproot them. In order to renounce, first we must pick out these negative things within us that do us no good and that have to be thrown away.[2]

This is such a powerful teaching, so simple, so direct, sheared of all embellishment. Sometimes, something that is so straightforward can go unheard and unseen. Something that is so pertinent can be rejected inadvertently.

As you blaze the trail to the place of tranquility within you, you learn how to strengthen yourself, how to develop patience and courage. And this means being flexible, letting go of things you don't need. For example, if you are going to climb a tall palm tree, you cannot hold objects in your hands. There may not be anything wrong with these things *per se*, but in this situation you must have your hands free. You need your entire being to hug the tree and move up the trunk in order to reach the fruit at the very top. Likewise, in *sādhanā* you must learn what to let go of and what to hang on to, and when.

Renunciation is not so much about giving up material things or traditional roles. It's not about giving up friends and family members, or comfort, or the duties of one's life. Renunciation is the way you balance the state of your own mind. And the sweet fruit of renunciation is equipoise. It is in the letting go that you receive the light of inspiration. It is in true dispassion that you feel the pristine Self shining forth.

Before that can happen, you must educate your mind. It must be taught to detach itself from the dumping ground of modern life: The dungeon of thoughts, concepts, opinions, gossip, fantasies, and futile imaginings. The fascination with outlaws and wrongdoers. The appetite for muckrakers who feed the obsession to see great people dragged down into the mud. The careless disregard for one's own good karmas. These are the things that the mind must renounce. Only then can it allow itself to open up enough to long for equipoise. Only then, when it is high enough above the chaos and the sludge, can it yearn to lose its pettiness in the great wonder of the divine luster.

Remember, you can make the year 1995 a stupendous one. You can occupy yourself with the highest thoughts. You can walk a luminous path, which will lead you to the resplendent world of the Beloved. In addition to all the acts of kindness and warmth that come naturally to a human being, think of how much more you can do. As wonderful as it may be to ameliorate someone's anguish by uttering a kind word, why stop there? Don't you want to go beyond the limits of the old familiar territory? Goodness is a natural part of every living being. Wouldn't you want to go even further than that? *Blaze the trail of equipoise and enter the Heart, the divine splendor.*

Do not forget, you have been presented with the year 1995 as a trophy for the time you have lived on this earth. It is your hard-earned merit, and you deserve it. A whole year, an uncarved block, still fresh and new, has been placed at your disposal. What will you do with it? On the one hand, you are fortunate to receive such an illustrious present. On the other hand, you have been entrusted with an awesome mission. What tremendous hope has been placed in your custody!

Right now, let's do a short exercise. Think of yourself as a master jeweler. One day, out of the blue, a person of great distinction puts before you a pure gold brick of startling proportions and says, "You are such an honorable jeweler, so well-known for your craftsmanship. I have complete faith in you. Please shape this brick into any form that inspires you. I'll be back after 365 days. And I hope by that time, you will have finished a piece of matchless beauty, worthy of your preeminence. Then I will reveal to you something that will transport you to a world of glory."

You, as a respectable jeweler, have been freely entrusted with a mighty venture. With what equanimity will you commit yourself to this task? How will you begin to give a form to the formless, to move with the creative energy, the divine

Śakti, and let Her dance through the shapeless brick, turning it into a breathtaking work of art?

Think about it. How will you, a skilled and gifted jeweler, respond to the power of such unrestricted freedom?

Will you maintain your equilibrium and bring a masterpiece out of the unknown? Will you simply go for it fearlessly? Or will you start to place conditions on it, such as the length of time allotted and the other obligations you have, the many commissions that are still waiting to be completed? Will you try to buy more time? What will you do? Will you ask to use just part of the gold now and save the rest for later, who knows when? How will you deal with this priceless offer, as well as with the trust that has been invested in you unconditionally? Will you embrace it? Will you blaze the trail of equipoise and enter the Heart, the divine splendor? Or will you fumble and freeze? What will you do?

A modern author once said:

> What we do on some great occasion will probably depend on what we already are, and what we already are will be the result of previous years of self-discipline.[3]

During the last Christmas retreat, I had a dream. I found myself speaking to a group of beings who were not from this world. I asked them the following question: "How can I truly convey the experience of joy, and of living in joy, to the people of this earth?"

One of them said, "It's not that easy!"

No sooner had he said that than there appeared an incredible manifestation. It was shaped somewhat like a long tunnel. At the end of it was an extraordinary and beautiful radiance.

One of the beings asked me, "Can you see the very farthest point where that brilliance is? That is the abode of joy. We all had to travel such a long, long distance to reach that place. When you get there, you discover that it is not a place at all, but a state. Can you imagine how far away it is? Can you imagine being there and trying to tell people here what the abode of joy is all about? Do you have any idea how difficult that is?"

With great respect, I entreated the being again and again, saying, "There has got to be a way. Even though the abode of joy is unimaginably far away, still you can see its light from here. That can give people great hope."

The divine being smiled and replied, "That is why those who have been to the abode of joy have to walk on the earth. They embody the bliss of that realm. They radiate its joy wherever they go."

Now is the time to begin: *Blaze the trail of equipoise and enter the Heart, the divine splendor.*

The first half of this Message, *Blaze the trail of equipoise,* urges you to follow the yoga of discipline. Every lofty endeavor that has been successful rests on the efforts — great and small — that people of strong hearts have put forth. Even the natural elements in this universe must play their part in the scheme of things. For example, earth, water, fire, air, and ether are unaffected by their own movements, as well as by everything that occurs in this cosmos. Yet, in and of themselves, they also perform their actions with constancy and steadfastness.

Bābā Muktānanda uses an analogy about the elements of nature in his introduction to *The Nectar of Chanting.* He writes:

> The seers say that *svādhyāya* — chanting and reciting sacred texts — should be performed every day with the unfailing regularity of the sun and moon, at an appointed hour, with deep feeling and reverence.[4]

Now perhaps this yoga of discipline, "the unfailing regularity," may not sound as spectacular as climbing the highest mountains. Blazing the trail of equipoise may not seem as adventurous as going to the moon in a rocket, or as exciting as scuba diving and eluding a shark who looks your way as it glides by. Equipoise may not sound as daring as camping on a mountain where bears roam at night, or sailing down the Amazon on a raft, or taking photographs of a war from the front lines. It's not as awe-inspiring as crossing the Sahara Desert on foot or taming a wolf.

Equipoise, you may think, is not as impressive as going on pilgrimage or fasting endlessly. Nor does it have the heroic allure of the ancient austerities. It doesn't sound as difficult or esoteric as standing on one foot for years on end. All these deeds may be incredible. They might deserve an award for outstanding achievements in the field of action. Don't you think they should be listed in the *Guinness Book of World Records*? But ultimately, what do they amount to? Even the most superb accomplishment cannot take you to the Heart if it is compromised by the desire for fame or name, affection, wealth, pride, and so on.

Why is that so? According to all the scriptures, one cannot achieve true greatness unless he or she can abandon all desire for recompense, for reward. This is the hardest thing to discipline oneself to do. But there is no way around it. As long as there is the slightest craving for praise from the world, all your actions are tainted with the impressions of *saṁsāra,* the world of delusion. Nothing obstructs equipoise more than this. Nothing so thoroughly blocks the way into the Heart and conceals the divine splendor.

How can you blaze a trail of equipoise without being overwhelmed by temptations and by desires, by the needs of every hour, the calling of every task? How can you find your way to steadiness of mind when you are riddled with the anxiety of keeping promises, the guilt of having performed prohibited actions, the gnawing pain of having deserted your only child, of having abandoned the life-saving spiritual path you were given, of having turned your back on the luminous golden disk of God's presence?

Even if your situation is less extreme, how can you reach the state of equipoise without dropping your constant need for attention — whether it is conscious or unconscious?

Stop for a minute and think of all the incredible demands you make. You demand to know your Heart and to experience its virtues. You complain about not seeing the wondrous effulgence within. And yet, you can hardly drop your wish for recognition for one minute. You meditate two days in a row, and you want to see the light of the Heart. You are so busy expecting greater and greater rewards for every tiny, insignificant action that you perform. And at the same time, you wish to realize the divine splendor. You are so caught up in the pursuit of compliments, acknowledgment, and expressions of appreciation that there is no time left in the day to pursue your quest for the luminous world of the Heart.

How can these things go hand in hand? It is a mockery. It is impossible. You have to drop your tendency to run after the fruit of your actions or you will always be frustrated in your supreme longing for the *darśan* of the radiant Being.

What is the answer? It is very simple and it is very direct: the yoga of discipline. It can make you strong enough to resist what must be resisted, to aspire to that which is worthy, to long for that which must be sought, and to renounce all the superficial things that must be eschewed, forgone. The yoga of discipline removes all these dark tendencies. It dissolves the small self with its limitations. It purifies you. It makes you transparent so that the light can shine through you. The Heart, the divine splendor, becomes your dwelling place.

Allama Prabhu was one of the most revered of the South Indian poets. His sublime poems preserve the power of his inner experience in words that are both precise and mysterious. He said:

> Light
> devoured darkness.
>
> I was alone
> inside.
>
> Shedding
> the visible dark
>
> I
> was Your target
>
> O Lord of Caves.[5]

Deprive your small self of the trivial, fleeting satisfactions of *māyā*, the world of illusion, and allow the experience of pure love within you to stream forth. Renounce the undesirable tendencies of the mind, yes! But hold fast to the company of true devotees. Drop everything that weighs you down, but protect and nourish all the things in life that uplift you. This is the trail that you must blaze within yourself. Let yourself be captivated by the luminosity of the inner world. Continue to strive for the highest goal of yoga.

Sādhanā, blazing the trail in a disciplined manner, gives you access to the state of equipoise, which is not easily understood and not easily attained. Then you continue to develop and draw on this profound equilibrium, this unshakable balance, through all the upheavals of daily life.

You continue your pursuit of the ultimate Truth without letting a moment slip by unnoticed. Your mind, like your time, is filled with the greatest virtues that a human being can embody: determination, perseverance, courage, patience, concentration. You are able to perceive each instant as a harbinger of good. You treasure every second as a shimmering jewel. You allow yourself to swim in a delightful ocean of laughter. Within, you experience something exquisite; it can only be called ecstasy. Then every moment brings you a full measure of God's glory. There is no limit to the heights you can reach.

In the closing chapters of the *Śrīmad Bhāgavatam,* Lord Kṛṣṇa gives many sublime teachings on steadiness of mind, equipoise, in what is known as the *Uddhava-Gītā.* He says:

> The person of steady wisdom should not swerve from his path, even though he may be oppressed by people who are themselves under the sway of destiny — this is the trait I have learned from the earth.[6]

Each individual is governed by his or her own destiny. Therefore, you must be very vigilant not to come under the influence of the consequences of other people's actions. Don't you know? When a boat is anchored in the bay, if it comes loose from its moorings, then any gust of wind or ebbing tide can carry it far away, out into the ocean, never to be found again.

To enter the Heart and perceive divinity, you must obey the rules of your spiritual path. If you do not remain faithful to your path, to the teachings of the Masters of your lineage, if you deviate from the Truth, then you become so lost. It is extremely difficult to get back to where you were, let alone make progress. And in the sea of *saṁsāra,* the sea of worldliness, your mind grows cold and dark.

How can you restrain yourself from falling into forgetfulness? Keep the mind hovering within the radiance of the Heart. Remember to lead it to the path of equipoise. Let it always glow with the warmth of that majestic light. *Blaze the trail of equipoise and enter the Heart, the divine splendor.*

To nurture the experience of the Heart, you must allow the disciplines of *sādhanā* to protect you. The state of equality consciousness, seeing the One in everything, gives rise to unearthly joy. To grow in that experience, you must perform your *sādhanā* diligently: continually listening to the wisdom of the great beings, contemplating the great truths that you have heard, meditating on the deeper meanings of the teachings, and also translating them into your daily actions. This is the path to even-mindedness.

Once you enter the Heart, you make a promise to yourself to live a life of *dharma,* a life dedicated to your highest duty. Having the vision of the divine splendor also means making a commitment to protect its sanctity. In this holy domain, which is your true home, you are open to receive the uninterrupted blessings of the Lord.

In the Indian scriptures, every new attainment is regarded as the occasion for renewed vigilance. It is a very particular attitude. When the yogis come to the realization of some divine aspect within, they don't become haphazard or unfocused. In fact, they celebrate an attainment by protecting it, like a miser guards his wealth, like a bird watches over its little ones. So then, how do you protect the mind that has just developed a new awareness of equipoise? You treat the mind with gentleness. Be as gentle as possible. Just as a newborn baby must be handled with the utmost tenderness and care, so you must watch gently over a mind that has just been born into a new awareness, the awareness of equipoise.

Have you ever watched a mother bathe her newborn baby? Do you know how she nourishes it and keeps it warm? And how she watches over her tiny infant day and night to be sure it is breathing freely and safely? That is the same way that you must behave with yourself: being gentle and yet keeping an unbroken vigil over your awakened mind so its movements may be guided in the best direction.

You must blaze the trail of equipoise with resolute will. At the same time, you must be willing to be gentle with those who are walking the path with you, as well as with those who are not yet ready or prepared for it. You must always remember that everyone is worthy of your love and respect. It takes very little effort, yet it is the highest thing you can offer them. Definitely, you must do this. It behooves you to be generous with your time, your virtues, and your comforts. Share them with other people as if they were an extension of your own family.

Once a great Guru asked his disciples how they could tell when the night ended and day began.

One disciple said, "When you see an animal in the distance and you can tell whether it is a cow or a horse, you can be sure that day has begun."

"No," said the Guru.

Another disciple said, "When you look at a tree in the distance and you can tell whether it is a neem tree or a mango, then you know the sun must have risen."

"Not that either," said the Guru.

The disciples were mystified. They said, "Please, sir, tell us, what can the answer be?"

"You can be sure that day has begun when you look into the face of any man and recognize your brother in him, when you look into the face of any woman and see in her your sister. If you cannot do this, then no matter what time it is by the sun, it is still night within you."[7] *Blaze the trail of equipoise and enter the Heart, the divine splendor.*

When you perceive the light of your own Heart permeating the entire universe, you have the amazing experience of oneness. The mind is so astonished by this divine splendor that all it wants to do is lower its head in awe and follow the command of the Lord. The experience never leaves you. Everywhere you go, it is with you.

Whether you go from the waking state to the dream state, from the deep-sleep state to the transcendental state, or from one room to another, one office to another, one city to another, one nation to another, really, space is no longer a barrier for you. Neither are the units of time.

Perform all your actions with discipline, and renounce the illusions of the world. Cultivate a whole garden of virtues, and extend their beauty to your brothers and sisters. Every day, wake up to the divine splendor of your own Heart. As you work hard to bring about the state of equipoise, go through the day acknowledging the presence of this divine splendor. As you go to sleep at night, may the power of equipoise remind you of inner ecstasy. Then, let your mind be at rest. Let your body be at rest. Let your whole being bathe in light.

May you be joyful blazing the trail of equipoise. May you be triumphant in entering the Heart, the divine splendor. May you be blessed with infinite grace as you venture into 1995. May you be filled with love as you fashion this year to glorify the indwelling Lord.

Whatever happens, remind yourself of this: the Heart, the divine splendor, is your home and final destination.

This is the Message for 1995: *Blaze the trail of equipoise and enter the Heart, the divine splendor.*

With great respect, with great love, I welcome you all with all my heart.

Sadgurunāth Mahārāj kī Jay!

Be filled with enthusiasm and sing God's glory

Siddha Yoga Message for the Year 1996

WITH GREAT RESPECT, WITH GREAT LOVE, I welcome you all with all my heart.

Another wondrous year has begun, the year of 1996. What does it hold for us? What does it intend to give us? What great magic will 1996 reveal? What destiny will it unfold before our eyes? Where will 1996 lead us? What treasures does it contain? How will it affect our lives? Is it the harbinger of good news? What will it bring with it? Will it bring our resolutions to fruition? What do you think? You must have been wondering what the year 1996 carries in its womb for you.

There is another way to look at this: How are you planning to welcome the new year? Have you prepared yourself to receive 1996 in the most auspicious way? Instead of pinning all your expectations on the new year, have you thought of doing something about the way you greet the future? Are you prepared to let bygones be bygones? Are you completely ready to take a new step forward?

The followers of Siddha Yoga teachings like to know at the beginning of each new year if there is a particular message for the whole year that they can imbibe and put into practice.

Siddha Yoga is the yoga of grace, the abundant grace of the Master. Freely and spontaneously this grace enters the lives of seekers. Yet for the Guru's grace to unfold in its fullness, it demands that seekers put forth a sincere effort to reach the goal of their seeking. Therefore, the Message for this year calls for both benevolent grace and sweet effort. The New Year's Message for 1996 is *Be filled with enthusiasm and sing God's glory.*

Enthusiasm dances in the bloodstream of the great saints and sages and all the true leaders of the world. Enthusiasm enables a person to realize his goal. Enthusiasm makes you soar. When you become aware of your own great capacity for enthusiasm, you realize there is something sacred within you. Why is this?

The answer is contained in the word itself. If you trace it back to its roots, you discover that the word *enthusiasm* comes from the Greek *enthusiasmos.* The syllable *en* means "in," "within," or "possessed." And *theos* means "God." So the word *enthusiasm* literally means "carrying God within" or "possessed of the inner Lord." When you are filled with enthusiasm, you are filled with the energy of God, with great power, with amazing grace. To become fully conscious of what you are carrying inside is to inherit all of heaven. This awareness frees you completely from worry. You are filled with God. What can possibly dampen your spirit? This new understanding of the word *enthusiasm* evokes a deep longing within you.

The question is, how can you make this divine quality stream forth within you? By singing God's glory. When you sing God's glory, you become filled with enthusiasm. And when you are filled with enthusiasm, then you sing God's glory as spontaneously as water flows in a stream after a bountiful rainfall. Each part of the New Year's Message is complete in itself, and each one also leads to the other.

In his book *Play of Consciousness,* Bābā Muktānanda says, "Enthusiasm and energy are very helpful friends in this world."[1] You must have noticed how you are spontaneously drawn toward people who are enthusiastic. When someone is full of exuberance and vigor, you want to be around them. Which one creates greater *rasa,* a greater flavor of life: the sight of a dry withered leaf or a fresh green leaf? If you see a depressed person and a happy person, which one of them generates a feeling of newness inside you? If you come across a gloomy face and a happy face, with whom do you want to talk? If you have a choice between two conversations — one that is depressing, sullen, and argumentative, or one that is filled with energy, laughter, good will, and eagerness — toward which conversation will you gravitate? There is an inherent impulse in every human being to move forward to a place, to a person, or to a time that is sparkling with enthusiasm, with God's energy.

To be filled with enthusiasm means to give yourself completely to God and let God steer the wheel of your life. Everyone wants his or her life to be full of purpose. In fact, many people ask, "What is the purpose of my life? How can I know the purpose of my life?" Everyone is looking for a way to live that is meaningful, dedicated, and full of wonder, *camatkāra.* Everyone wants to be full of happiness and love, to lead a harmonious life with great friends, sweet pleasures, a feeling of abundance, and great wisdom, uninterrupted by loss. Everyone really does want all this.

However, most people seem to look for meaning outside themselves. They think that abundance, purpose, and pleasure are hiding somewhere else in the world, and they need to go and hunt for them. They forget that each human being is the pivotal factor in his or her own life. Each person holds within himself that which he is seeking. In order to make your life the way you want it to be, you have to become filled with enthusiasm. You have to become the perfect vessel to carry the golden light of grace.

You don't have to leave it to fate to decide what the coming year will hold for you. If you make the best of each moment, then 1996 can become the greatest and most wonder-filled year of your life. *Be filled with enthusiasm and sing God's glory.*

Once, in response to a seeker's question, Bābā Muktānanda said:

> Whatever you acquire in the outer world will ultimately leave you weak and feeble. There is only one thing that will make you stronger day by day, which will release more and more enthusiasm within you, and that is the Guru's grace. As you pass into meditation through your Guru's grace, you find your life becoming sweeter and happier.[2]

To visualize enthusiasm being released within you through the grace of the Guru is a great *dhāraṇā,* a centering technique.

Bābā was always filled with enthusiasm. That was one of the things that drew people to him. Enthusiasm poured out of Bābā — when he was in the kitchen cooking, when he was playing with a child or talking to people, when he was looking at the ocean or giving a scholarly commentary on a scripture, when he was studying alone at his desk, or when something was humorous. Just as the ocean roars, enthusiasm roared within Bābā. Whether he was watering a plant or giving instructions to a sevite, whether he was gazing out at space or sitting quietly in the courtyard, you could experience unbounded enthusiasm streaming from him, washing you clean, filling you with a sense of the glory of life. You felt life moving inside you when you watched him, whether he was in action or just sitting quietly.

When Bābā strolled through the gardens or sang the name of God, when he gave profound advice or greeted a visitor, you could feel his unimpeded enthusiasm, the exuberance that was dancing within him. Whenever you caught even a glimpse of his brilliant orange robes on the other side of the upper garden of Gurudev Siddha Peeṭh, our mother *āśram* in India, you felt a tremendous flood of enthusiasm pouring out of him. From the first thing in the morning till the last thing at night, Bābā's entire day was lived with enthusiasm. He was always bright-eyed and brightly smiling. His entire being pulsated with great wonder. When you saw him, you wanted to know more about life. Enthusiasm is what Bābā taught. He would say, "Do your work with enthusiasm. Chant God's name with enthusiasm. Let there be enthusiasm in your being." Bābā's enthusiasm was contagious. To be with Bābā was to be full of Bābā's joy.

Let your entire year of 1996 be filled with exuberance. *Be filled with enthusiasm and sing God's glory.*

A scholar of Kashmir Shaivism, commenting on the teachings of the sage Utpaladeva, writes, "Wonder is the essence of life. To be incapable of wonder is to be as dead and insensitive as a stone. We live and enjoy the vitality, *vīrya,* of Consciousness to the degree in which we are sensitive to the beauty of things around us."[3] Each aesthetic experience should be enjoyed mindfully and with a disciplined intention. This intention is directed toward heightening the general level of our sensitivity to beauty. In that way, every bit of beauty that you encounter will bring you a little closer to a sustained sense of wonder. This wonder is the pulsation of Consciousness that permeates all experience. The scholar continues his commentary, "A yogi at first practices to penetrate into this state of wonder through the medium of objects more easily pleasing and then, as he makes progress, he learns to discern that same sense of wonder in himself, even when confronted with the foulest of things or in times of great trouble and pain."

This is what Bābā Muktānanda continually taught us. Whenever we got upset as young children, Bābā would call us and say, "Look! Isn't this stone beautiful!" And we would look at the object and think, "A mere stone." He would say, "Look, this is so beautiful!" We looked at him and looked at the stone. And then he would laugh, and within a few seconds we would be laughing, too. As soon as we started laughing, we could see that the stone was in fact so beautiful. Bābā showed us the great wonder in simple things. And he completely changed our mood, our way of thinking, by infusing great wonder into these simple things.

After we received *śaktipāt*, we found out that people can have dramatic experiences if they continue meditating. But we noticed that our meditations weren't that deep or dramatic. We were just sitting quietly. So we became a little restless and we walked around the *āśram* with long faces. We felt our meditations weren't really going that well. Bābā would unfailingly find out what we were feeling. You see, the *āśram* was very small in those days and Bābā had an invisible magnifying glass — at least that's what we thought. And so he invited us to come to the courtyard where he was sitting, and he asked, "How's your meditation going?"

Of course, we weren't eager to describe our meditation experiences. So we just sat there and looked at him.

He said, "Your meditation is great?"

Finally, we said with downcast eyes, "No."

"No? Your meditation is not good? What do you mean? When do you meditate?" Bābā asked lots of questions, and we tried to answer them as well as we could. Then he said, "That's wonderful! You are so fortunate! You are so lucky!"

We thought, "Really? Just to be able to sit quietly is wonderful?" We had never realized that. Just to sit quietly is meditation. That really is a great attainment, just to sit quietly for a couple of hours. We became infused with this novel idea that to sit quietly for two hours without going anywhere was a dramatic experience.

Bābā continued to say how wonderful it was and how fortunate we were, and we completely melted into his enthusiasm

— about our boring meditation sessions. And then we went back to our daily meditations with so much enthusiasm. In fact, we woke up singing because we were so happy to go and sit for meditation — just to sit quietly for a couple of hours.

So you start with simple things, and then you carry your enthusiasm to greater and greater realms. You carry the wonder-filled attitude into every moment, into every action, and you experience your own boundless enthusiasm.

As a true seeker you must develop this sense of wonder. Everything in God's universe is a cause for wonder. You must be able to experience awe and respect for all the forms of life around you. Then you will be able to maintain your enthusiasm. This means never feeling dull or at a loss, never feeling lethargic or defeated, never feeling helpless or betrayed, never feeling dead or deserted. When you go to work, go with a sense of wonder. "Oh, how is the office going to be today? Who will I meet today? What conversations will take place? What wonderful work is waiting for me?"

When you contemplate in this way, enthusiasm comes and presents itself before you. When you go to meet someone, have this sense of wonder. "Who will I meet? How will the meeting be? What will be the outcome?" Don't walk into the office thinking, "Do I really want to see that woman's face again? Oh, so much paperwork. What will I do?" No! Go to your office eager to find out, "How many more projects can I look into? How much more paperwork can be put in order? What is the best way to accomplish the work?" And when you go shopping, don't disparage everything on the shelves. Let the market be filled with wonder. "Those artichokes — aren't they wonderful! That cashier — isn't she nice! The person over there, she's my neighbor. I'll go help her. She is always so kind to me." And when you are driving somewhere, instead of dreading all the traffic, find ways to create a wonderful *satsaṅg* for yourself. "I hope I don't have to drive too fast, because I want to listen to this new chanting tape. I hope I have a lot of time in the car to chant all the way."

A little child constantly experiences wonder. Everything about life tingles and activates curiosity in the being of a child. Children come into this world with an inner smile and eyes that want to grasp the magic of the universe. Being with children, parents relive their youth, whatever their age may be. This sense of wonder, which is the essence of life, continually creates fresh life. *Be filled with enthusiasm and sing God's glory.*

You can fill your entire year with enthusiasm. Begin now by welcoming the year with your whole heart. Who knows? It may be filled with wondrous teachings, magical insights, marvelous experiences and encounters. Whatever it brings, adopt a yogic attitude and discern the same sense of wonder within your own self. Whatever the year presents you with, remember to sing God's glory. Keep the name of God on the tip of your tongue. Relish its ineffable beauty. Let 1996 be the most wonder-filled year.

Welcome this sense of wonder into every aspect of your life. When you first wake up in the morning, greet the day with praise: "*Sadgurunāth Mahārāj kī Jay!* What a glorious, grace-filled morning! What a wondrous feeling I have inside! *Oṁ Namaḥ Śivāya!* Awake I am! May the entire day be filled with God's wisdom!" Visualize the happy face of your Guru. Hear the strains of the mantra echoing inside you. With great wonder, look forward to what the next moment will bring. Visualize every cell in your body filled with vitality. As Bābā Muktānanda would say, "Vitality is coursing through every blood corpuscle." Let this vitality assist you, let it see you through the day.

As you breathe in and breathe out, become filled with more and more enthusiasm. God's glory is flowing in your veins. God's glory is singing through all your actions. Let this energy guide you throughout your day. Do not judge whether what you are doing is impressive or mediocre, spiritual or mundane. Just do it with enthusiasm. Just give yourself to whatever you do with this full knowledge: "God is within me. All actions that I perform are offerings to Him. Whatever He wants to do with me, let Him do it as He wills." Have the certainty that God is with you, that you carry God's energy, and that all your actions are in praise of Him. Walk happily. Speak sweetly. Do everything diligently. Be meticulous in every dealing. Let *dharma* support you.

Bābā Muktānanda used to say:

> Always remember your own inner Self with great love. Always think of the dazzling flame of love that is present inside you. That flame will fill you with great delight, great happiness, great zest.[4]

How do you experience this dazzling flame of love? Through singing God's glory. This doesn't mean just sitting in one place and chanting the name of God. Singing God's glory is allowing your entire being to send forth God's beauty, God's bounty, God's love. You must let God's energy flow into every minute of your day. That is singing God's glory.

In the *Rāmāyaṇa*, Hanumān, the great devotee of the Lord, says, "Any moment spent without singing God's name and glory should be regarded as a great loss. That moment is a moment of ignorance and delusion."[5]

Singing God's name is singing His glory. Chanting the mantra is singing God's glory. But isn't there another, even more meaningful way to sing God's glory? Isn't there another means that is very pleasing to God? Yes, there is. There is a splendid path by following which you truly do sing God's glory. To experience God's perfection in all the people you meet is to sing His glory. When you meet people, instead of sizing them up and down, look for the great virtues they carry within them. Begin to appreciate every little thing they do. That will make it easier for you to recognize the great things they are capable of. Allow yourself to acknowledge the goodness you see in each person. That is singing God's glory.

When you see a beautiful plant, let yourself feel its loveliness and thank God for its existence. When you see the sun rise and set, let yourself be engulfed by its majesty spreading across the sky. Watch it display the most unearthly combination of colors — each sunrise unique, each sunset unrepeatable. Thank God for the existence of the sun. Understand that each one of your days is just as incomparable and just as heavenly.

When you see the stars and the moon in the night sky, let yourself be overcome by tender feelings and thank God for their existence. When you receive compliments from others, let them warm your heart and thank God for His grace in that form. When you are afflicted with troubles and unexpected calamities, thank God for their existence, too. Know full well that He will protect you and that He wants you to extract a lesson or two from them. That is singing God's glory. When you expect people to do something for you and they don't come through, feel good about them anyway.

Don't change your good opinion about them. That is singing God's glory. When nothing seems to go the way you want, continue to maintain your inner composure, your inner delight, and offer your gratitude to God. Perhaps God wants it some other way. That is singing God's glory.

God's power is *śrī*. It is filled with auspiciousness, beauty, sacredness, abundance, nobility, dignity, and good fortune. When you allow your actions to be suffused with these qualities of *śrī*, you are singing God's glory.

When you allow your good understanding and virtues to guide your words and actions, rather than letting your attention be led away by lack of understanding, then you are singing God's glory. When you take the time to speak with someone who is seeking spiritual upliftment and tell her about your inner experience of God's love and grace, you are singing God's glory. When you recognize unconditional love flashing forth in someone's smile, in a gesture of kindness, in his steady helping hand, in her cheerful spirits, don't let the chance slip by. Take a moment to express your love. This is singing God's glory.

When someone awakens great love in your heart, don't just keep it for yourself, thinking, "Oh, her love is meant just for me." Acknowledge such a loving nature. That is singing

God's glory. When you meet someone who has worked very hard for the benefit of many people, who has given his or her best to the world, don't presume that your appreciation is immediately felt. Take a moment to express your gratitude, your heartfelt appreciation. This is magnifying God's beauty, God's abundance, God's sacredness. It is spreading good fortune everywhere and singing God's glory.

Whenever your actions express the inner magnificence of the Heart, the inner auspiciousness, the inner spiritual power, you are singing God's glory. *Be filled with enthusiasm and sing God's glory.* This is the Message for 1996.

Right now, in this very moment, you can allow yourself to experience an ocean of enthusiasm and the continuous pulsation of God's glory in your own being. You can experience your Self. Just become aware of your body; your own being carries the energy of God, enthusiasm. You don't have to wait for the circumstances to be impeccable and perfect. You simply make a decision: "I am going to let God's energy pour through me. I am going to make all the space in my heart, all the space in my being, available for God. I am going to walk through the day and night seeing God's presence everywhere around me and allowing His energy to work through me." Let the sense of wonder be constant. It's just a simple resolution.

Remembering God is singing God's glory. Repeating His name is singing His glory. Seeing God in each other is singing God's glory. Respecting God in each other is singing God's glory. Understanding and worshiping God in each other is singing God's glory. Loving God in each other and being generous with each other is singing God's glory. Showing kindness to each other is singing God's glory. Expressing gratitude to each other is singing God's glory. Then in turn you experience His rewards as great enthusiasm, zest, and ecstasy.

When enthusiasm courses through your veins, when music dances in every cell of your body, you become a beacon of light for this world. Everyone around you is happy — automatically. You don't have to roam from continent to continent trying to fulfill yourself. Fulfillment is already yours. You carry the vessel of fulfillment. Then wherever you go, you have something to offer others. This is singing God's glory.

In his book *From the Finite to the Infinite,* Bābā Muktānanda says:

> This is why we live: to experience supreme bliss, the highest enthusiasm, the highest ecstasy. A human life is mysterious and significant; it is sublime and ideal. In this human body, in this human life, we can see the

> Creator within, we can meet Him and talk to Him, and we can also become Him.[6]

Sit quietly for a few moments and visualize God's energy coursing through your entire body. The body has its own subtle vibration that you can experience. You may feel it on your skin or deep in the marrow of your bones. When you allow your entire being to become still in its own subtle vibration, you can experience God's power. It is *śrī*. It is filled with auspiciousness, beauty, sacredness, abundance, nobility, dignity, and good fortune. Know that all this exists within yourself.

Give yourself this gift throughout the year. Experience your own *śrī*, your own auspiciousness, your own beauty, your own sacredness, your own abundance, your own nobility and dignity, your own good fortune. Let every virtue in you blossom. Let every hidden good quality of yours shine forth. Immerse yourself in your own *śrī* and emerge with the blossoms of *śrī*. *Be filled with enthusiasm and sing God's glory.*

With great respect, with great love, I welcome you all with all my heart.

Sadgurunāth Mahārāj kī Jay!

WAKE UP TO YOUR INNER COURAGE
AND BECOME STEEPED
IN DIVINE CONTENTMENT

Siddha Yoga Message for the Year 1997

WITH GREAT RESPECT, WITH GREAT LOVE, I welcome you all with all my heart.

The birth of a new year is an awesome experience. And in only three years, we will have the birth of a new century. The beginning and the end of a great cosmic fragment — a thousand years. Time is on an eternal journey. It is tireless, invulnerable, powerful, yet utterly detached. Time is beyond suffering. It flows with constant delight. Look at its play. It is detached, but it is always experiencing delight.

You have already made a resolution to welcome 1997. What agreements have you made with yourself? For example, have you resolved to respect all the blessings that spring out of your own being in every moment of your life? Time carries a promise: to inspire you to perform actions that are pure and to lead a life that is full of purpose.

This is an auspicious moment. We are standing on the cusp of something new and wondrous. Such moments are filled with sparkling possibilities. Let us welcome the year 1997 with great enthusiasm, with great affection, with true love.

The Siddha Yoga Message for 1997 is *Wake up to your inner courage and become steeped in divine contentment.* These two great qualities, courage and contentment, go together. One is born from the other.

In the *Bhagavad-Gītā,* courage is exalted. It is described as one of the attributes of God Himself. In chapter 11, after Arjuna has seen the vision of Lord Kṛṣṇa's cosmic form in all its terrifying grandeur, he cries out:

> Salutations to You from in front and behind,
> salutations to You on all sides, O God of all.
> You are infinite valor and boundless might.
> You pervade all, therefore You are all.[1]

In the Sanskrit language, the word *vīrya* means "valor, courage, heroism." It is a term that one often finds associated with God. The words *santoṣa* and *tṛpti* refer to "contentment." This quality is also celebrated as a very high attainment in the scriptures of the Indian tradition. Listen carefully to what the *Kulārṇava Tantra* says:

> There is no mantra higher than meditation, no god higher than the Self, no worship higher than the inner pursuit, and no fruit greater than contentment.[2]

May 1997 be the year in which you wake up to your inner courage and become steeped in divine contentment. May you wake up to the presence of God within you and savor the bliss of the state beyond desire. May you have the courage to embrace life fully.

Originally, you came to this earth plane knowing there was something you could attain only here and nowhere else. You knew this with absolute certainty. You took birth on this planet, realizing that you have something to offer, something you could accomplish only here and nowhere else. Your being on this planet is a choice you have made.

For just a moment, think of a particular place you have always wanted to visit. Or think of a place where you have always wanted to live. Does one spot leap to your mind right away? Why? Because it holds something special for you. Isn't that true? Something meaningful. Because you believe that place will reveal something important and give you the life you are looking for. In the same way, your being on this planet is a choice that you have made. Whether you still agree with it or not, whether you are able to come to terms with it or not, whether things are going well or not, you have made this choice. If you perceive this life as a choice — as your choice — it is easier to see how full of amazing wonders it actually is.

To have this enlivening perception, recognize that you have the courage within you to fulfill the purpose of your birth. Summon forth the power of your inner courage and live the life of your dreams.

Do you step lightly upon the earth or heavily? On the whole, are the things that come before you full of smiles or frowns? What about your possessions? Do they bring you happiness or unhappiness? Are the people in your life helping you to make greater progress or inhibiting your growth? How much of that is up to you? More than you think! Whether you feel you are winning or losing ultimately depends on the way you approach things and the way you let them approach you.

Courage is not just a response to crisis; it is not just a sudden act of bravery in a fire or a war. And contentment is not merely the sense of satisfaction that comes after you get everything you want. Whatever happens in your life is for your own upliftment. Fragrant, delicious fruit is hidden within every occurrence of every kind. Have the courage to find the best outcome in every situation. *Wake up to your inner courage and become steeped in divine contentment.*

Whatever the adventures or challenges of life may be, you are the one who has the power to decide how you want to look at things, which way you want to turn your head. Even the best news in the world can bring you down if you insist on it. Your own being in its totality approves or disapproves of your existence on this planet. You hold the reins. You have a choice.

Courage is such a simple word, and yet at the same time it is multifaceted. It holds many other great qualities within itself. Strength, generosity, kindness, hope, love, learning, acceptance of life, and gratitude — these are all a part of courage.

True courage must stem from the depth of your being. It is yours. Courage is the very membrane that shields your heart. Courage is what fends off negativity and transforms adversity into growth. Its undaunted power can pierce through the distracting pull of the senses and make a miracle happen. In fact, courage attracts miracles. Truly, a life of courage is filled with miracles.

Is courage always easy to feel? Easy to spot? Not really. Sometimes courage is invisible. Yet courage is an inherent part of you, it is natural to you. It is really you — you are courage. Courage is you. However, just to wake up to the presence of courage inside you takes tremendous courage. It's not like waking up after a nap or a good night's sleep. Waking up to your own courage is actually a matter of waking up to the light of the Truth, to the light of supreme Consciousness within you. An awakening like that demands your firm determination and the touch of grace.

The light of the Truth is infinite. How are you going to actualize it in all its vast magnificence? The best and most efficient thing you can do is to follow one particle, one strand, one ray, of this infinite light. You can follow it by articulating it in language. Then you can begin to discover that the experience of divine Consciousness is within your grasp.

For now, we are following the ray of light emanating from this beautiful and powerful word, *courage. Courage* — what a sweet word. *Courage* — what a strong word. *Courage* — let us follow its light all the way back to its source, to the splendor within the Heart.

As the Sūfī master Hafiz said:

> Come, join the courageous
> Who have no choice
> But to bet their entire world
> That indeed,
> Indeed, God is Real.[3]

Wake up to your inner courage and become steeped in divine contentment. Even when you just repeat these words to yourself, "Have courage," you dive into the ocean of your own inner Self and emerge as a new being, dazzling with light. To express the dauntless spirit of inner courage takes a whole new language, and it is good to see this quality in a new light — the light of 1997. With this new language and new vision, allow every moment of your life to pulsate with courage and contentment.

There is a famous character called Sheikh Nasruddin. He knew that courage and bravery were very important, and therefore he faithfully attended an annual conference of daring hunters. He loved to go there and listen to people speak about feats of bravery.

One year a hunter stood up and said, "I got hold of the tail of an elephant and twirled him around in the air!"

Another man declared, "I killed a wild tiger with my bare hands."

A third recounted to the group, "With just the power of my gaze, I held an entire pack of rabid hyenas at bay!"

Finally, it was Nasruddin's turn to speak about his most glorious and heroic moments. "Once I pulled out the horn of a wild bull — just like that! Another time I grabbed hold of a huge snake and snapped it into two pieces — just like that! Yet another time I knocked a crocodile unconscious!"

"Wow! Wow!" everyone cried. "What else happened, Nasruddin?"

"What else? I had to run for my life!"

"Really? What happened?"

"The owner of the toy shop was coming after me with a stick!"

The courage that we have been empowered with, that we want to discover, is not like Nasruddin's empty boasting. That is the kind of courage some people exhibit when they are merely showing off. They want you to imagine that they are courageous. However, there is real courage within you, and you must wake up to it.

What are some of the other ways that weakness masquerades as courage? Courage is not about breaking the rules to prove to others that you can do exactly what you want. It is not about inviting suffering into your life either, just so everyone can see your unflinching devotion to God. Having courage is not a question of passively accepting everything that happens. To have courage does not mean shrugging your shoulders, or sighing, "What can I do? It's my karma."

On the contrary, having courage means engaging in every single situation as a blessing from God, as a loving gesture of nature. Courage means rising to meet the demands of each moment with total delight, knowing you are equal to it. Courage means having faith that within you is an innate force whose essence is never depleted by external events. Live your life courageously, dharmically, knowing that whatever you are faced with is not stronger than you are. You are equal to each other. Your problem is not greater than you are, nor is it smaller. This approach is a dharmic way of living. This is courage. You look at your problem as your equal, never greater or smaller. And therefore, you can rise to the demands of each moment. With great delight you are able to face and accept whatever comes your way.

Everywhere you look, throughout the history of the world, you find wonderful, heartrending stories about courage. You come across stupendous tales and incredible anecdotes. They fill you with the desire to live courageously. They *en-courage* you. What's more, the same sorts of events that are written in those tales are also taking place right now. At this very moment there are people who are revealing their vast inner reserves of courage. They are saving the world in both large and small ways. Their benevolent thoughts are full of the light of courage, and this makes their resolutions firm. They have become beacons of courage for others. Right now, all this is happening.

Recognize your inner courage. You have it. You may already be a living hymn to courage. And this is as it should be. The infinite light of the Truth must definitely be translated into everyday life.

I love reading the books of my Guru, Swāmī Muktānanda. I love to read his great writings, his wonderful and divine teachings. I turn to them again and again. They are my *prāṇa,* my life force. His wisdom is my courage. His wisdom is my life. I continually relish what he has written, what he has given to us. The messages of great beings are timeless. Their messages are inspired by the infinite light of the Truth, the supreme

Reality, and therefore they always hold something new for you. Their wisdom resonates completely with your own inner knowledge, with everything that life has taught you.

However, messages don't come only from the great beings. A message that calls out to a willing heart can appear anywhere. For example, you can hear messages even during the simple conversations and occurrences of daily life. No matter how casual the words may seem, they can still hold a message of Truth, of absolute wisdom. Such a message removes the thick veil from any situation. If you are stuck, a message is a priceless gift that can turn you around.

In every moment, you can find a great message. A playful dog you meet might convey a message of joy and fearlessness that allows you to solve a very difficult problem you are facing. A weed growing beside the footpath can hold a message. The deep sorrow in the heart of a friend also holds a message for you. There may be a pebble in your shoe that is annoying you, yet its presence might hold a message that wakes you up to your inner courage. The sight of moonlight streaming through a window may hold a message that reminds you of the infinite splendor of God. Everyone has access to this place of blessings; you just have to turn to it and listen. Listen to the messages that life provides.

Now, what kind of messages and blessings are you really seeking? Suppose you are walking down a wintry road and you are freezing. You know your destination is not far away; however, it is cold. You are losing confidence. The wind is ferocious. Your footing is precarious. The air is so icy, it hurts to breathe. And you begin to feel you won't make it. Just then, someone sees you stumbling and invites you into his house. He gives you a hot cup of tea and a warm blanket. This good neighbor rubs your hands and feet to get the circulation going and revives you completely so that you can go on. That is wonderful. Who wouldn't be grateful for such kindness?

But there is a downside to this much-needed help. Because if the same thing ever happened to you again, you would be looking for someone to save you. But you might not happen to receive the same loving treatment. You can't always count on being rescued. This kind of help may be a one-time thing.

Now, instead of being offered a hot cup of tea, suppose you come across another sort of help — a person who knows the road and knows how you truly feel. Suppose that friend says, "Have courage. You can do it. Have courage. You are almost there. Look! Your destination is right there!" The warmth of his voice and the certainty emanating from his heart give you the full strength of his blessing. The complete assurance in his voice is like an infusion of energy. The power behind his statement stays with you — "Have courage" — and helps you reach your destination. "You can do it. Have courage. You are almost there."

And when you arrive, what a splendid experience! You have discovered not just your destination — you have discovered your inner courage, and it has brought you to your goal. By waking you up to your inner courage and by giving you faith in your own ability, this true well-wisher gives you a lasting gift. If the same type of incident happens again, you will remember, "Have courage. You can do it! Have courage. You are almost there. Look! Your destination is right there." The message is the lasting gift. You will experience God's blessing, God's grace, very strongly.

Waking up to your inner courage makes you self-reliant. Once you call on this courage, you recognize it for what it truly is: you see that courage is an exquisite spark of the infinite light of the Truth. And when you call on this divine light, the power of God at the core of your being takes you across. Having courage is invoking God's power within yourself.

Knowing this, Bābā constantly urged people to avail themselves of all the strength they carry around inside themselves. He said, "You should have courage, you should have purity, you should have bravery, you should have enthusiasm, and you should have the feeling that you can accomplish everything."[4]

That is the simple truth. Let it fill you with the joy of fearlessness. You can accomplish everything! *Wake up to your inner courage and become steeped in divine contentment.*

You may be encountering this message during a pause in a busy day, or at a moment when you need to make a clear and firm decision about your career. You may be engaging with this message at a *satsaṅg* in a Siddha Yoga meditation center. You may be reviewing this message the last thing at night as you enter the magical world of dreams — dreams of courage and contentment. Or you may be contemplating this message as you embark on a brand-new life. Therefore, discover this virtue in your own being.

What a magnificent feeling it is to wake up to the presence of your inner courage. To realize that wherever you are, you can actually perceive the brightness of life with your own heart. By waking up to your inner strength, by calling on the virtues of your inner being and putting them into action, you make your heart even stronger. You recognize the divinity that abides in the heart. It does take courage to embrace Bābā's teaching: God dwells within you as you. See God in each other. To understand this fully, you have to wake up. You have to wake up to your inner courage. I have heard it said that courage is not the absence of fear but the understanding that other things are more important.

Of all the virtues of spiritual life, courage may be the one that the world finds easiest to recognize. Every nation admires the spirit of courage. As you know very well, the world does not respect cowardice. No one ever wants to extol a person who cringes before the challenges of life or flees from duty. You don't respect yourself, either, when you are filled with fear and the desire to quit. Cowardice weakens everything you stand for, everything you believe in. Cowardice has to be one of the worst feelings. Like a deadly poison, it eats away at your mind and spirit, killing you slowly at the very moment you are fighting hardest to survive. It takes courage to strive for the highest. It takes courage to turn your senses within. It takes courage to seek the supreme Self, to seek out the inner worlds. And therefore, right now, resolve to let every moment of your life be filled with the enthusiasm of courage and divine contentment.

In the lives of all beings, there is occasion for strife. Does that mean you should give up? Does that mean you should allow your weaknesses to parade around and tell everyone how feeble you are? Is that the way God sent you to this earth? No. He prepared you in heaven. He instilled you with courage. He said, "You want to go to the earth because there is something you want to learn there, because you have something to offer there. Go with My full blessing." And how did you feel when you first decided to join everyone on this planet?

Why not think of that moment of courage? You came to this earth with courage. Why do you want to hide it now and go around making people feel sorry for you, making them feel pity for you? Is that the way to serve God? Is that the way to recognize God's presence in everyone?

Cowardice makes everything more painful. It doesn't matter whether you are talking about war, work, or life in general. Cowardice hides behind a veil of false courage and lures you toward destruction. When people are smoldering with anger, resentment, or envy, they say, "If only I had the courage to tell that person what I really think about him!" Can you see how cowardice is hiding behind a veil of false courage here and luring you toward destruction?

What are the other impulses that come up involuntarily when you are in the grip of your emotions? What are the fantasies? When you are stuck in a traffic jam, have you ever wished you could step on the gas and just plow through the cars in front of you? Is that courage? Wishing you were bold enough to tear up all your bills and go to another city and start a new life? Wishing you had the courage to hit the person who makes you so angry?

Foolhardiness and outbursts of anger do not display the kind of courage we are talking about. We are talking about releasing the goodness of your heart. This form of courage is never used as a weapon. It is never called upon to destroy life or to show off.

Where does this courage really come from? Think about it. We are following this ray of light to its source. The scriptures say emphatically that selfish desires involve you in things that deplete you. So courage must arise from somewhere else. It has to come from a place beyond desires, a place where desires starve to death, a place that is rich in wisdom and wholeness.

That place is called contentment — the deep sense of being in the great Heart of God, the knowledge of inner fulfillment. Contentment — understanding what is yours and what is not yours, knowing that all of it belongs to God, and resting in this knowledge, taking repose in this wisdom, the supreme peace of the Heart.

Courage has a very strong relationship with contentment. Not the temporary kind of contentment you experience when you quench your thirst or satisfy your hunger. Not the easy satisfaction of mind that can be bought by soothing words that feed your ego. Not any of the promises of comfort that other people make. Here we are talking about divine contentment, in which you experience total surrender. Why? Because you are strong. You surrender not because you are weak; you surrender because you are strong.

As a philosopher once said, "Contentment is a pearl of great price, and whoever procures it at the expense of ten thousand desires makes a wise and a happy purchase."[5]

Between them, courage and contentment bring your world into balance. The poet-saint Akka Mahādevī, who lived in India in the twelfth century, once said:

> Having been born in this world,
> you should not lose your temper
> at praise or blame,
> but maintain the poise of your Heart.[6]

Always, Bābā Muktānanda maintained the poise of the Heart. He was steeped in the peace of the Heart. Being around him filled you with the same kind of peace and contentment. During his second world tour, Bābā told a group of seekers:

> There is no wealth like contentment, no health like contentment, no husband like contentment, and no wife like contentment.[7]

Like courage, contentment is not a passive virtue. In divine contentment, you are not merely pretending to be at peace. In fact, it is a continuous *tapasya*, a wonderful struggle, to "maintain the poise of your Heart." Such a beautiful phrase from the poet-saint. But what exactly does it mean to struggle to maintain the poise of the Heart?

Why should the heart's well-being take any less effort than the body's well-being? Just as you are attentive to what you feed your body and how you care for it, in the same way you have to be careful what you feed your soul and how you tend to it. It requires steady, quiet effort to keep the heart producing the *rasa,* the sweet flavor, of contentment. You don't just sit back and think, "I don't need anything. Whatever will be will be. *Que será, será.*"

Once you taste contentment and start to live in its beauty, you actually want this river of grace to overflow its banks. Living in such contentment gives you the courage to march forward and make the most of this gift of life — life, which is full of difficulties and expectations, full of glory, challenges, promises, purposes, rewards, and failures; life, which is liberating, which lets us create our freedom; life, which is the gateway to enlightenment.

Bābā once said, "Contentment destroys ego."[8] This is a fascinating statement. It may seem startling to hear that such a benign quality has so much power, that contentment can actually eliminate the most powerful obstacle of all — the ego. Isn't it like hearing that the softest flower petal can blunt the edge of the sharpest sword? Or that one tiny leaf from a rare herb can cure a malignant disease? Or that a slender green vine can cut a huge mountain in two? It may sound far-fetched to think that something so small and soft, so delicate and fragile as contentment can obliterate something so big, resistant, and impregnable as the ego.

But then, Bābā wouldn't say such a thing unless it met four requirements. Bābā insisted that spiritual teachings be based on personal experience, backed up by the scriptures, supported by the words of great beings, and finally, blessed by one's own Guru. Therefore, we can be sure that contentment does destroy ego. Contentment is that soft and that powerful. It is truly the most brilliant, life-giving *rasa* there is.

When Bābā says, "Contentment destroys ego," this thought-provoking phrase creates a stir in the womb of your knowledge. It begins to breathe new life into your understanding. It animates anything that may have become stagnant or complacent. It makes you move.

Even the slightest bit of contentment has a powerful effect. Haven't you found that the sweet smile of a baby can melt your heart, no matter what you are going through? Wouldn't you be enchanted by the sight of the morning sun reflected in a dewdrop, even if your heart was heavy? Haven't you heard that one sip of water can revive a person who has fainted? Contentment does destroy ego.

What will happen if you let yourself steep in divine contentment and draw your courage from there? It will save you from the enemies of your mind that eat up the serenity of your soul.

Where can contentment truly be found? Contentment arises from knowing that you are with God and God is with you. This experience must be constantly renewed. Then your contentment is always fresh like the dawn and new like the beginning of each year. Again and again, remind yourself: "I am with God, and God is with me. I am with God, and God is with me." *Wake up to your inner courage and become steeped in divine contentment.*

I had an amazing dream. In this dream I was swimming in the ocean with several devotees, as well as some lions and tigers. We were all having a lot of fun. Suddenly, someone shouted to me, "They're coming! They've started!"

We looked up and saw a series of gigantic waves on the horizon. They were still far away, but they were approaching us rapidly. They were huge; they must have towered at least two hundred feet in the air. Everyone else was a terrific swimmer, but I was not. I didn't know how to ride the waves at all. I had no chance of getting away. The waves seemed to gather speed as they approached, and as they came closer, they looked even bigger. I made the decision that the best thing to do was to let go completely and allow myself to slip beneath the waves as though I were lifeless. I consciously began to surrender to the ocean. I became completely serene, still, and weightless, so the ocean could wash over me and do anything it wanted to do with me. From deep within, I knew this was the most courageous thing I could do — to remain in this state of tranquility, in this state of meditation, and resist the temptation to struggle.

In that state of total peace, I could still hear the others crying out, "They're coming! They're coming! The waves are coming!" All at once, the giant, towering waves started crashing down upon us. Everyone struggled to stay above water. Eventually, all of them managed to ride a wave and get out of there.

I was alone under the tumultuous sea. Yet, I did not feel the least bit helpless. I was in a deep state of tranquility, a deep state of meditation. My entire being was suffused with total surrender to the ocean and absolute contentment in this surrender. It was my choice. I had made a decision to consciously surrender and just be there. After a long time, I found myself gently washed to the shore, completely unhurt. My state was unbroken. It was the most profound, blissful experience of being totally protected. Spontaneously, from deep inside, these words arose: "I am the daughter of the ocean. I am the spirit of the ocean."

Everyone was so excited that I was alive. Then we looked around and saw that one of the lions, who had also washed up on the shore, was lying there in excruciating pain. It looked like his back was broken. This lion had thought he could fight the waves and beat them in a big display of courage and strength. But now he lay there suffering terribly. He could hardly move. We went and stood by him.

Seeing us, he said, "All of you, learn this lesson from me. I wasn't hurt by the ocean. I was hurt by my own pride."

Whenever you think you are helpless, you are denying God's grace and the Guru's blessings. The minute you turn to the source of grace, the minute you turn to the infinite light of God in your heart, you find the peace and all the protection you need.

There is a beautiful *bhajan* written by a lover of God, who sang about the Heart as an ocean. It goes like this:

> How can waves on the surface affect
> one who is seated in the depths?
> What can outer events do
> to one who is complete in himself?
> How can an ordinary person understand
> that this contentment resounds
> with the most amazing things?[9]

May you go to sleep at night filled with the power of courage and experience the sweet flavor of divine contentment. May you wake up in the morning with courage and experience the sweet flavor of divine contentment.

May you apply yourself to spiritual practices with the enthusiasm of courage and experience the sweet flavor of divine contentment. May you devote yourself to your family duties with the inspiration of courage and experience the sweet flavor of divine contentment.

May you follow the discipline in your life with the strength of courage and experience the sweet flavor of divine contentment. May you rise to the needs of every moment with the light of courage and experience the sweet flavor of divine contentment.

May you live the life of your dreams with the energy of your inner courage and become steeped in divine contentment. May you fulfill the purpose of your birth with the illumination of courage and become steeped in divine contentment.

May the year of 1997 awaken you to your inner courage and give you this benediction: become steeped in divine contentment. May you wake up to your inner courage and become steeped in divine contentment.

With great respect, with great love, with enormous love, I welcome you all with all my heart.

Sadgurunāth Mahārāj kī Jay!

REFRESH YOUR RESOLUTION.

SMILE AT YOUR DESTINY.

Siddha Yoga Message for the Year 1998

WITH GREAT RESPECT, WITH GREAT LOVE, I welcome you all with all my heart.

A very Happy New Year to you all. *Feliz año nuevo! Bonne année! Nayā sāl mubārak. Nūtan varṣa abhinandan.*[1] Happy, Happy, Happy New Year to you all.

It's begun! We've crossed the threshold. Here we are in the moonlit new year of 1998. It's so new. It's so bright. It's so transparent. It's so tender. It's so caring. It's so mysterious. It's delightful. It's promising. It sparkles with good humor. It is iridescent. It is melodious. It is precious. It carries deep wisdom — the moonlit new year.

When the year actually changes, what happens? We, too, travel with time. Time is such a great revealer, such a wise teacher, such a glorious asset. Time is a sweet companion, and a scold. Time is a lover. Time is a secret. Time is the most ancient sage. Time is ever playful, ever open and expansive. Time, the great equalizer, resonates with the Truth.

It is wonderful to travel with time. When you flow with time, you are not rushing toward the next event. You are not always thinking there is something better waiting just around the bend. Nor do you drag your feet, trying to cling to memories of the good old days. When you are in sync with time, you know you are in the right place, at the right time, and with the right people. When you move with time, your wisdom grows to immense proportions.

Once upon a time, we woke up to our inner courage and became steeped in divine contentment. We tasted its nectar. We relished it. We drank to our hearts' content. We became so immersed in the delicious pool of contentment that 1998 came like a silky jasmine breeze and whispered, "I am here." And it was true! We opened our eyes and found ourselves in the moonlit new year.

On the whole, I would say we rose to the occasion. How did we do it? With the sound of God's name. We could feel it approaching from the depths of our being and vibrating through our lips — God Himself in the form of sound. Is it fire? Is it nectar? Is it velvet? Is it emptiness? Is it just what it ought to be? How can we describe the way God's presence makes itself felt? A great Sūfī saint sings:

> O Lord, You are my goal and You are my destiny.
> You are my only aspiration and my heart's desire.
> Everyone worships You, because You are the One
> who is truly worthy of reverence.

Those who are blinded by ignorance
are convinced that You don't exist.
But those who have the eyes of wisdom
proclaim God is alive, You are alive.
They have seen You, O Lord.

Why should I beg from anyone?
What can anyone else give me,
when my Lord, my great Lord, gives me everything?
My Lord gives me everything
with His unseen, invisible hands.

You have such unique artistry in Your hands, O Lord.
You can create anything.
You give each one of us our life and You nurture it.
Therefore, I have put my faith in You alone.

Friends, don't embroil yourselves in petty concerns.
Absorb yourselves in chanting.
Soak your mind in God's name.
Then even the hardest times
will not be able to dampen your spirits.

If He bestows just one compassionate glance upon you,
then not only will you be uplifted,
in that moment your entire destiny will change its course.
O Lord, You are my goal and You are my destiny.[2]

The moonlit new year — it is so refreshing, is it not? It is already full of your resolutions, is it not? And your smiles, too. It makes your destiny intriguing, does it not? Ahh, moonlit new year, you are bound to make us better than the best. You are eager to stretch our limits, to make us reach the zenith of our aspirations. Will you unite our hearts? Yes. You are prepared to draw us closer to God. Then, moonlit new year, what message do you hold for us?

The Siddha Yoga Message for 1998 is *Refresh your resolution. Smile at your destiny.*

This Message comes in the form of an expanded poem. You can think of it as a *dhāraṇā*. In Sanskrit, the root of the word *dhāraṇā* means "holding or placing something in the field of your awareness." The word *dhāraṇā* implies that which flows into the space within yourself, a place that is intimate and familiar and filled with unexplored possibilities. The scriptures call this space supreme Consciousness. So let your heart become a vessel to contain these words. Let your heart be completely open as we journey together through this poem.

The ancient Indian scripture called the *Atharva-Veda* says:

> The person whose resolution is firm knows that the powerful Lord dwells within all beings and hears everyone's prayers. To one who inwardly offers himself to his resolution, the Lord happily gives the inner strength and equanimity to endure all hardships with a sublime and peaceful smile.[3]

Refresh your resolution. Smile at your destiny.

With each new beginning comes a natural desire for change. We respond by setting a new direction. And so we make a resolution, a shining promise to ourselves. However, it cannot stop there. Every resolution, large or small, requires effort. It can be realized only if this effort is sustained. It needs your attention on an ongoing basis. Every resolution has to be carried out with resolution. When this is not the case, you make resolution after resolution, resolution after resolution, resolution after resolution — you have an ocean of resolutions crashing on the shores of daily life, littering your mind with broken promises.

You see, a shining resolution that is not honored will not disappear. It stays in your awareness. Like driftwood in the waves or a blinding flash of light on the water, it's always moving around trying to catch your attention. You know it's there. You become aware of your inability to act on it. You see your laziness, lack of strength, and negligence. You try to make it go away. You come up with a hundred million excuses for why you aren't willing to fulfill it. But it won't go away, because you have given life to it. There has to be some resolution about it, even if you don't want to fulfill it. Otherwise, you are the one who is going to be eaten up. Sooner or later, this leads to an atmosphere of hopelessness and helplessness.

Cynicism, lack of worth, lifelessness, lack of strength: all these forms of unhappiness show up when your resolution stagnates. In this way, little by little, a person succumbs to the spirit of darkness. Therefore, it is vitally important to understand the nature of resolution.

To make a resolution is to decide on a course of action with firm determination. What impels you to make a resolution? Why do you make a resolution? Basically, there are two answers to this question: the impetus either comes from the outside or from the inside. For instance, you may decide to make a resolution because you have noticed something in your community, in your parents, or in your friends. You may have accepted standards of how to be, how to eat, what to weigh, and how to care for your body — and you resolve to achieve these goals. Resolutions like this can be positive and very sound. They can improve your experience of life if you embrace them in a sane way. Or your resolve may come from inside yourself, as a vision of your deepest wish, your sweetest dream. When you make a resolution, it is a way of drawing this secret wish into the light of your awareness and putting it into action so that your life increasingly reflects God's love, God's essence.

Whether your resolutions are practical or lofty, what matters is how you hold on to them. For a resolution to have power, you must hold it so close to your heart that it is almost like a secret, almost a prayer.

The ancient *Ṛg-Veda* says:

> May you awaken like the sun at daybreak,
> ready to make your sacred offering.
> Set forth with delight, like a pilgrim on his journey.
>
> O heroic one, move forward with resolve
> to make this sacred offering of yourself to life.
> May you plant the banner of victory
> in the service of humankind.[4]

This prayer is charged with resolution. Can you hear it? Can you see it? Can you feel it? Also it conveys the fact that this resolution has to be refreshed every day. The sun never rises the same way twice: the color of the sky, the angle of light, even the heat are all unique. And yet the whole earth is renewed; that never changes.

To have the image of waking up at dawn like the sun recharges your entire being with the fresh smell of the morning earth. You can just see the birds darting out of the trees, out of the rocks, out of the bushes and flying across the rising sun, chirping. You can hear the ringing of bells at the hour of morning prayer. This is such a fulfilling way to begin the day, with the *Guru-Gītā.* It infuses the entire body with life-giving energy. Then we put that energy to use in the most beneficial way possible: in *sevā,* in the service of humanity. Refreshing your resolution — this is what enlivens resolutions that may have gone dormant. They are just sleeping, you see, waiting for the dawn. Remember: refresh your resolution.

The *Atharva-Veda* says that one whose resolution is firm knows that the Lord dwells within all beings and hears everyone's prayers. Just hearing that — the Lord hears your prayers — just believing in that is so refreshing. To the person who inwardly offers himself to his resolution, the Lord gives the inner strength to endure all hardships with a sublime and peaceful smile. Of course, the sages have taken a royal road, a golden path. They had the vision of God within everyone, and their experience became their resolution. See the power in their resolution. Their experience became their resolution. Yet, even this must be refreshed. You can never become lackadaisical about the highest Truth. Like the morning sun, your resolution has to be new every day. Its colors must blaze brightly.

Nature is a master at this renewal. She knows just exactly how to refresh herself, how to rejuvenate her seeds and revamp her paradise. She refreshes herself through storms, torrents of rain, floods, brushfires, volcanoes, and earthquakes. These are the most dramatic displays of the ways she renews her being. But the same process also happens on a smaller scale, like a snake shedding its skin, the trees dropping their leaves in the autumn, or a bear hibernating. Think of the way the winter snow covers the ground like a blanket; it seals in the earth's own heat so that seeds can germinate underground. Or think of an even subtler level of renewal. Think of the dew, the nightly perspiration that moistens the earth. Think of the mist rising off a lake, or delicate showers. Or think of the fact that while most of the herbs grow by the light of the sun, others are nourished by moonlight. It's amazing, isn't it? The food that sustains our life draws on all the different lights of day and night. Nature is absolutely gorgeous in her liveliness. You want to know beauty? Observe nature. That is because she constantly refreshes her resolution and, in so doing, she refreshes the entire universe.

The fruit of refreshing your resolution is as plain as day: the energy of the entire universe supports you. You have a clear vision of the purpose of your life. You are filled with the breath of self-confidence. You experience your fresh young spirit. You make progress. Your self-esteem heightens. Listen to the fruit of your resolution: You flourish. You are bursting with inspiration. You glow with optimism. You become radiant. For you, life is dazzling with newness.

A genuine resolution continually spreads its delight all around. Why? Because it is born out of love. Does the same thing happen when a resolution is prompted by selfish motives? Not really. When a resolution is saturated with hostility, when it is spawned by bitterness or fueled by resentment, when a resolution breeds in a swamp of inferiority, then you won't even see the shadow of ecstasy. You will not be able to experience one ounce of gladness from it. Such resolutions must not be refreshed. They should be burned in a funeral pyre. Let even the seeds burn completely to ashes. But a resolution that upholds what is noblest in life deserves to be honored. It brings strength and serenity to the one who keeps faith with it. *Refresh your resolution. Smile at your destiny.*

There are a hundred million ways of going about this — renewing the power of your resolution, creating a transformation in your deepest commitments and convictions. Be resolute! Brighten up your resolution. Restore the positive energy in your resolution. Light a fire under your resolution.

In India when a resolution is made — before, during, and after — you invoke *śakti,* the divine Power. First, you create an environment of sacredness and blessedness. Then, you let your resolution manifest in the most auspicious way, streaming from the inside, from the Heart into speech. Then, you allow it to be absorbed by the holiness of the divine Power. Finally, you ask for protection, you ask for the strength to sustain this resolution and live up to its merit and its excellence. Can you see the hidden force in your resolution? By verbalizing your resolution in the presence of grace, you give it a true and fresh life. That moment stirs the soul. It is like receiving initiation, *dīkṣā*. You are making a resolution, and you are also receiving *dīkṣā*. A resolution that is born out of a humble, sincere heart produces a rich and bountiful harvest. Such a resolution must not be forgotten. It has to be refreshed over and again. It has to become like the morning sun, bringing new life to every single day. Refresh your resolution.

Bābā Muktānanda once said:

> If you really want to advance on the spiritual path, you have to be very firm, very resolute, and very disciplined. If you leave yourself loose, you will fall very quickly.[5]

Everyone knows that when a bone becomes brittle, then any little accident will break it. It is no different with inner work. The way to keep your spiritual life strong and supple is through firm resolution. Otherwise, carelessness seeps in and eats away the merits of your good actions, your *puṇya karma*. Your *puṇya karma*s are eaten up. Before you know it, you begin to lose interest in the very things that bring you good fortune. You become indifferent to the spiritual practices that make your life meaningful. You get bored with people of good will. You distrust your friends, your good friends, who only wish for your well-being. You look upon every divine sign with suspicion. You become deadened to nature, which is the source of your life. You waste away the thousand and one boons that you have received from God. All this happens, let me tell you, very gradually, imperceptibly. You scarcely notice it. However, when your resolution becomes shaky, weakness filters into every aspect of your life.

What can you do to avert these possible disasters? Refresh your resolution. Understand the impact of a resolution. Come to see how even the simplest resolution breathes new life into you. For instance, you may have made a resolution to follow the road to good health. You may have made a resolution to take your family on a holiday when *they* want to go. You may have made a resolution to speak sweetly to others. You may have made a resolution to support good causes. You may have made a resolution to see the bright side of life. You may have made a resolution to increase your devotion. You may have made a resolution to do at least one spiritual practice a day.

You may have made a resolution to give *dakṣiṇā* regularly. You may have made a resolution to see God in everyone. You may have made a resolution to experience God's protection in everything. These examples are about enhancing your life and bringing greater meaning to it.

Another approach is when you make a resolution to refrain from certain actions. You may have resolved to break the habit of constant arguing. You may have resolved to put an end to your tendency of comparing yourself with others. You may have made a resolution to stop misunderstanding Lakṣmī, the goddess of wealth. Some of your resolutions may be about trivial, everyday matters, or they may be about things that are deeply meaningful to you. You may be embarrassed about some of them, even if you never tell a soul. Therefore, it is very important to look at each resolution through the eye of the Heart. Ask yourself: How does it go down? How does it sit inside? What is that deep feeling? Is it putting you at ease? Or is it creating havoc? Look at it from the eye of the Heart. It will tell you the truth. Yes, the Heart tells the truth.

Of course, every resolution is bound to be important to you. Otherwise, you never would have thought of it. So you must honor your resolutions, every one — small or large, pragmatic or cosmic. Whether you are praying for self-improvement or for all of humankind, your resolution matters. Never give it up. Jalal al-Din Rumi, the great Sūfī mystic, says:

> Come, come, whoever you are —
> wanderer, worshiper, fugitive.
> It doesn't matter.
> Ours is not a caravan of despair.
> Ours is a caravan of endless joy!
> Come — even if you have
> broken your vow a thousand times.
> Come, come yet again. Come.[6]

This is so refreshing — the call of Rumi. His words are as alive now as the day he first wrote them. And every time you read them, they give you fresh encouragement. The truth is, you must never despair. No matter how many times you have to pick yourself up and start over, just do it. Rumi said, "Ours is not a caravan of despair." Trust his words. Believe him. "Ours is not a caravan of despair." How could it be? We have entered the moonlit year and it holds eternal spring. Remember, it's so new. It's so bright. It's so transparent. It's so tender, so caring, so mysterious. It's delightful and promising. It sparkles with good humor. It is iridescent. It is melodious. It is precious. It carries deep wisdom — the moonlit year.

Refresh your resolution. It is like taking a dip in the Ganges at dawn and welcoming God in the form of the sun, the glorious sun. In the same way, dip your resolution in the refreshing, nectarean teachings of the scriptures. Learn to remember God. Learn to rethink each thought. Learn to reshape each action. Learn to reexamine your own heart.

Learn to renew your understanding of what you have heard. *Refresh your resolution. Smile at your destiny.*

Bābā Muktānanda says, "One creates one's own destiny." That is a very remarkable statement. One person is born blind, another poor; another has to share his mother's womb with six other siblings. Yet, Bābā says, "One creates one's own destiny." What can he possibly mean? Bābā continues:

> We create our own heaven and our own hell, but we hold other things responsible for it, such as our country or our government or our destiny or our parents or the planets or the scheme of things. We become friends with one person and keep swaying in the joy of that friendship. We become hostile to another person and keep rejecting him all the time inside ourselves. But it is we who have created that friend, that enemy.
>
> Therefore, change your way of looking at things; make it divine. We meditate so that we may be able to see the world as it really is.[7]

If, as Bābā says, you are the creator of your own destiny, then why not create it with a smile? If you are the experiencer of your own destiny, then why not experience it with a smile? If you are the owner of your own destiny, then why not own it with a smile? Bābā says, "Change your way of looking at things; make it divine." Then why not look at things through the eye of the Heart? Isn't that where the divine dwells within us? If you perceive things in this way, you will have an irresistible impulse to smile. And guess what? It will brighten up your destiny.

Destiny and *smile* — both of these words are buzzing with nuances, connotations, histories, different interpretations, philosophical arguments, centuries of pessimism and optimism — the field is very crowded. *Smile* and *destiny* — they are highly debatable. They have been put through fiery tests, and yet they remain an absolute enigma. Nevertheless, your destiny continues to fashion and refashion your life, and so does your smile.

A Spanish proverb says, *Todo el mundo sonríe en el mismo idioma*: "Everyone smiles in the same language." Just think of all the ways a smile has affected you — because, of course, everyone knows there is more than one way of smiling. A smile can send your spirits soaring. A smile can be an expression of wisdom, welcome, playfulness, innocence, joy, compassion, and benevolent grace.

It is one thing to receive a warm, approving smile from someone you care about very deeply, and quite another thing to receive a smile from someone who hates you, who is sarcastic, scornful, and cold. That smile can cut you to the quick. In fact, a smile can be a way of showing aggression, like animals baring their teeth. What other kinds of smiles do you come across? Flirtatious, knowing, embarrassed, plastic, nervous, mischievous, and vague. And then there is the famous smirk. There is no doubt that every type of smile has played a part in creating your destiny. However, in the end it doesn't matter what people think about the subject of destiny; it *is* created.

Whether destiny is glorified or criticized, garlanded or reviled, or simply denied as a force in the universe, its basic principle is at work all the time. The truth is so simple, it is crystal clear: every action has a reaction, every cause has an effect. This is what keeps the vicious circle going. Whatever it is called — karma, destiny, fate, coincidence, chance, or luck; *el destino, bhāgya, prārabdha, niyati, adṛṣṭa, kismet, naseeb* — it is all the same. The naming ceremony doesn't really matter. What must happen does happen, irrespective of one's intelligence or foolishness, one's money or poverty, one's stinginess or generosity or rank in life. That is just the way it is. Goodness breeds goodness; evil breeds evil. This has been proven in every age and in every culture.

Therefore, why not greet your destiny with a genuine smile, a smile like Bābā's, a smile that will smooth the hard edges of destiny and empower you to move in a direction that evokes auspiciousness, *maṅgala.* A genuine smile truly opens the heart.

Describing the way nature smiles, an author once said, "Laughter is day and sobriety is night, and a smile is the twilight that hovers gently between both — more bewitching than either."[8]

The bewitching smile. Truly, nature abounds with enchanting smiles. It is our duty to learn from her. We must allow our being to absorb her offerings, so that we can give back to the universe all the golden presents that we have received, so that we learn generosity. In the Indian tradition, in both word and image, the Lord is represented with a smile playing on His lips. It is an expression of His bliss, out of which the whole world is made.

Benevolent grace always smiles. Therefore, the *Śrī Sūkta* describes the awesome power of the Devī, the Śakti, God's own energy, saying:

> The nature of the Goddess surpasses the mind
> and lies beyond words of mortal speech.
> Her face is lit with a beautiful smile;
> Her body is radiant with golden light.
> She is compassionate and generous.[9]

In the same way, verse 92 of the *Guru-Gītā* says:

> The Guru has a gentle smile *(manda-smita)*.
> The Guru is joyous.
> The Guru is a treasure house of abundant grace.[10]

Manda-smita — the gentle smile, the soft smile, the tender smile, the caring smile, the benevolent smile. Bābā Muktānanda writes beautifully about the smile of his Guru, Bhagavān Nityānanda:

> Lost in supreme bliss, his face was always illuminated with a radiant, sweet, and compassionate smile. From time to time, he would laugh, and that laughter still echoes in my memory. Because he loved to smile, people came to address him as Nityānanda, one who is always in bliss.[11]

Bābā inherited his Guru's smile completely. By cultivating such an open, pure, and genuine smile, such a gentle and wise smile toward destiny, you are truly able to call forth your own inner divinity. Then, you will not be tormented by the hot winds of the opinions of this world. A true, genuine smile is like a cool breeze. It carries the seeds of serenity and ease and scatters them over the earth, where they take root. The destiny that grows from such a smile spreads its fragrance everywhere. Smile at your destiny.

Bābā says:

> One who has received true knowledge . . . considers destiny to be a mere game and lives life joyfully. He knows that all kinds of things happen in life and that the world is a vale of sorrow, but he does not worry about it. Destiny does not terrify him. He remains calm in the midst of difficulties and does not get bored if life is easy.[12]

Smile at your destiny. Isn't destiny the mystery of all mysteries? Different people have different approaches to destiny. Some people think that destiny steers their every move. Others think, "I control my destiny." Some people think that character defines destiny. You get what you are, so to speak. Others make themselves helpless victims of destiny. They think there is nothing they can do, and they give up right away. Some people resist destiny. For example, they have great things to share, but they withhold their love. Some people have an adversarial relationship with destiny. They think destiny is out to get them: "It's coming at me!" They blame destiny for all their problems. Still others refuse to believe destiny exists. But listen, destiny is knocking at the door. Whether you hear it or not, destiny opens the door by itself. Smile at your destiny.

Some people think destiny is a great teacher. There is so much to learn from it, they say. Some people actually want to work with their destiny to achieve fulfillment. Some people want to support others' destiny by being good to them. Some people have total faith in destiny. Some appeal to destiny for help. And the sages know they have a higher destiny, because they believe God dwells within themselves.

At any rate, destiny plays a very important role in everyone's life, believe it or not. Whether you try to face your destiny, dodge it, or deny it, destiny is there in one form or another. Therefore, in Siddha Yoga, we always like to refer to destiny as our great good fortune, *sadbhāgya.* We say, "It is my great good fortune that I have a Guru. It is my great good fortune that I have such wonderful people in my life. It is my great good fortune that I have a longing for God." By constantly addressing it with these exalted names — *sadbhāgya, saubhāgya, puṇya karma* — we are able to smile at our destiny. And in turn, it smiles at us sweetly and generously. Great blessings always come with a genuine smile. Bābā used to like the saying, "If you cry, you cry by yourself. If you laugh, the whole world laughs with you." In the same way, if you smile, you befriend the whole world. But if you complain all the time, you push everyone away. So by smiling at your destiny, you bring out the best in it. Then it doesn't matter what your destiny is — you bring out the best in destiny by smiling at it. And also, since every action has a reaction, smiling now plants the seeds of happiness for the future.

What do you think you will accomplish by berating your destiny? What do you think you will lose by smiling at it? Don't wait for a favorable change in your destiny. Smile at your destiny right now. Don't turn away from an unfavorable shift in your fortunes. Smile at your destiny. What you think is favorable may not be so great. What you think is unfavorable may be to your advantage. Therefore, smile at your destiny —

whatever form it takes. Always envision your destiny as a harbinger of good news. Think like that. Smile at your destiny. Smile. As Bābā says, "Be happy. Have great joy and bliss, and always smile." Make yourself a great giver of good fortune. Make yourself a refreshing lake. Make yourself an abode of fulfilling resolutions.

Refresh your resolution. Smile at your destiny. Take this Message to heart, and you will fill your year with songs and laughter, with sweet fulfillment. The touch of your smile will make every facet of your destiny shimmer like the colors of a rainbow. Keep yourself very fresh and very light. With a fresh young spirit, walk the path. With a fresh young spirit, walk the path. With a fresh young spirit, walk the path. *Refresh your resolution. Smile at your destiny.*

With great respect, with great love, I welcome you all with all my heart.

Sadgurunāth Mahārāj kī Jay!

A GOLDEN MIND, A GOLDEN LIFE

Siddha Yoga Message for the Year 1999

WITH GREAT RESPECT, WITH GREAT LOVE, I welcome you all with all my heart.

The ending of one year and the beginning of another puts a new perspective on our entire life. What would we do if time did not exist? How would we live? What measure would we use? When we are certain that time is going to keep revolving, that the earth will turn and the seasons will change, then we can experience balance in our lives. Then it does not matter whether we live in a place where the sun is shining all the time or we never see the sun at all. Time is still revolving, and we live by its rhythms: morning, afternoon, evening, night.

We are just beginning to bathe in the first light of 1999. How auspicious. We have welcomed it by coming together, chanting the *Guru-Gītā,* and having *satsaṅg.* What a sublime way of welcoming the first day of the new year. What a great way to open our beings to a new direction.

Let us make a resolution together. Let us embrace 1999 as a present from time, from God. Let us understand how valuable this year really is. It is a doorway to a brighter life.

In Siddha Yoga we have developed a tradition of gathering together for the unveiling of the New Year's Message.

When you hear the Message, I want you to know this is an initiation for the whole year. The power of the Message will infuse your understanding and efforts with grace. The Message for 1999 has been waiting silently on the cusp of the year, spreading its tranquility and increasing in radiance. Do you recall having heard that the most precious gifts come in small packages? Therefore, listen attentively. The Siddha Yoga Message for 1999 is *A golden mind, a golden life. Una mente de oro, una vida de oro. Svarṇim man, svarṇim jīvan.*[1]

Come, let us walk together on this golden path, at this golden time, in this golden company, to receive the golden fruit. Be with the Message. Stay with the Message. *A golden mind, a golden life.*

Right now, listen to a prayer from the *Ṛg-Veda.* It is an ancient scripture, which was divinely inspired. The sages experienced this scripture in one revelation after another. The *Ṛg-Veda* says:

O bright golden sun,
when you are born together with the dawn,
you make the golden light shine forth
where before there was no light.
Indeed! From the unformed darkness

you reveal the beautiful form
of this brightly colored world.[2]

In the same way, the *Kaivalya Upaniṣad* describes the experience of the Self. It is as though God Himself is speaking. In fact, in this Upaniṣad, God *is* speaking.

aṇor aṇīyān aham eva tad-van
mahān ahaṁ viśvaṁ idaṁ vicitram
purātano'haṁ puruṣo'ham īśo
hiraṇ-mayo'haṁ śiva-rūpam asmi

I am subtler than the subtle, greater than the most great.
I am this manifold and wondrous universe.
I am the ancient One.
I am the great Consciousness.
I am the golden hue.
I am the very form of Śiva.[3]

This golden light is always all around us. Every morning we are greeted with the golden disk rising out of the earth, over the ocean, over the hills, and over buildings. Every evening we are ushered into velvety night by the golden rays of the setting sun. As we move through the day, we are enveloped by the golden light from beginning to end.

The *Kaivalya Upaniṣad* says, "I am the golden hue." There is a Latin word *aurum,* which means "shining dawn." It is the source of the chemical symbol for gold. *Aurum,* the shining dawn. In fact, many things that we value, many things that we consider precious, we describe as golden. We speak of golden opportunities, golden anniversaries. We say that someone has a heart of gold. When we agree on a guiding principle of right conduct, we call it the golden rule: do unto others as you would have others do unto you. We call it golden, not just because it enunciates an eternal truth, but because we can apply it in every situation as a measure, a yardstick, for our own moral standards. And it will never fail us; therefore, we say it is golden. You have a golden heart. The Siddha Yoga Message for 1999 is *A golden mind, a golden life.*

Every seeker is looking for the essence of life, searching for life's enduring purpose. A seeker wants to find a way out of this maze. Instead of struggling endlessly to conquer life, or constantly getting ensnared by different ideas of life, a seeker — I mean a true seeker — wants to find the meaning of life. Who am I? What am I? What is this world? Why am I born? What am I supposed to do? Where do I go? What is life? What is death? A seeker wants knowledge, and also the experience that knowledge brings.

And yet, for all the striving and effort, life remains the mystery of mysteries. There are glimpses, perhaps, of greatness, and also of atrocities. Yet for the most part, life remains impenetrable, as if life has its own life.

What do you know about life for sure? Life is something that you have, you have been endowed with, and you cannot escape. Whether you take it as a treasure or a burden, you have a life. You have life. It is yours. That much is clear.

Is there, then, more to life? Yes. Can it be known? Oh, yes. To see into the heart of a subject as profound as life, you must have a very fine medium, a powerful medium, one that can reflect life in all its depth and diversity. That medium is the mind. When it is a golden mind, it perceives a golden life. *A golden mind, a golden life.*

Just as the earth is blessed with a golden sun, you are blessed with a golden mind. At face value, you may find it difficult to accept that your mind is so valuable, particularly when you are aware, when you are acutely aware, of the battle you wage with your mind, the endless conversation you have with it, the constant struggle to pull it back from destructive thoughts and wild fantasies. When you think of its yammering and clamoring and woolgathering and your vain attempts to reason with it, you might feel embarrassed to say that you have a golden mind. Or you might be afraid that it is arrogant even to entertain the idea, "I have a good mind." All this discomfort is mainly due to a simple lack of recognition. Recognition of what? Of the blessedness of the mind, of its essential nature, which is golden. In the *Kaivalya Upaniṣad,* the Lord says, "I am the golden hue." *Hiraṇ-mayo'ham.* "I am the golden hue."

Now, you may want to know how you can recover your golden mind, how you can reclaim the experience of blessedness of the mind. For a start, just think of gold. Did you know that gold itself can be hammered so thin that sunlight can shine through it? For gold to acquire its purest form, what does it have to go through? Fire. It burns in the fire, and burns in the fire, and burns in the fire. Then finally, the expert artisan recovers gold in its purest form. He must be very careful, though. Melting gold to get rid of the dross so that it can shine with its own luster, unobstructed, is no simple task. It is a complex and amazing process of transformation, one that is often used as a metaphor for yoga.

Let us begin the process of refining an understanding of the New Year's Message by turning to the *Bhagavad-Gītā,* one of the holiest books of India. It is a beautiful dialogue between Master and disciple, Lord Kṛṣṇa and Arjuna. No matter how disheartened Arjuna becomes, Lord Kṛṣṇa perseveres in imparting his teachings, again and again — one chapter, two chapters, three chapters, four chapters. He goes on and on; there are eighteen chapters in the *Bhagavad-Gītā.* Because of this, Arjuna finally overcomes his despondency and receives the power of the universe to perform his *dharma,* his duty. The *Bhagavad-Gītā* represents the *dharma* of the supreme Self.

In one of its verses, Lord Kṛṣṇa reveals something wondrous about the mind. In chapter 10, the Lord is describing His various manifestations. He says that among all things, He takes the form of what is highest and most great. In verse 22, He says:

> *indriyāṇām manaś cāsmi bhūtānām asmi cetanā*
>
> Among the senses, I am the mind.
> I am the Consciousness of all beings.[4]

"Among the senses, I am the mind." When Lord Kṛṣṇa says, "I am the mind," what happens? Doesn't that stop your mind? Doesn't the mind boggle at the thought? Why do you suppose that is? For a moment, look at your own mind. What benefit do you derive from it? What is the purpose of your mind? How do you display your own mind to other people? Are you driven by your own mind or are you the master of your own mind? Do you think of your mind as ordinary or special? Do you realize that your mind shapes your destiny, that your mind is what shapes your life? Minute by minute, thought by thought, do you realize your mind is what shapes your life?

In the Indian scriptures, a human being is considered to have eleven senses. There are the five senses of perception: the powers of hearing, seeing, smelling, tasting, and feeling. There are the five powers of action: the powers of speaking, procreation, excretion, handling, and locomotion. Now the

Lord says, "I am the mind." That, according to the Indian scriptures, is the eleventh sense. Though God is the power behind all our actions, here in this verse Lord Kṛṣṇa declares that the greatest and most divine of all the senses is the mind. The Lord Himself firmly takes His seat in the mind as the eleventh sense. *A golden mind, a golden life.*

The mind can be a vast field of liquid gold, undulating from one shore to another. You can become totally lost in its awesome power. On the other hand, your own mind can be the worst enemy you will ever have. It can lead you into a swamp. It can chase you up a tree. It can get you into a pretty pickle. It can run you ragged. It can send you around the bend. It can lead you to wrack and ruin. It can land you in the doghouse. It can send you to hell in a handbasket. So, the same mind can be friend or foe, gold or dross. And believe it or not, the choice is up to you. It is your choice. You are the one who makes your mind your friend or your enemy. You are the one who puts yourself on the good side or the bad side of the mind. You are the creator of the state of your life.

My Guru, Bābā Muktānanda, says:

> It is the grace of the mind that is far more important than anybody else's grace. You may enjoy the grace of

> all the other people that you know; but if you do not enjoy the grace of the mind, then other people's grace will not help you at all. You have to win the grace of the mind.[5]

Isn't that great? You have to win the grace of your own mind. *A golden mind, a golden life.* Here Bābā is revealing the power of your mind. He is beckoning you to have a real grasp over the mind. He is saying something so vital here: you have to win the grace of your own mind.

Take the example of gold. A huge chunk of gold ore is valuable even in its crude state. However, its value increases in the hands of an expert. Then it can be used to make ornaments. In fact, in medicine they use gold to cure diseases. In recent times, gold is used in technology. For gold to achieve its potential, the process of smelting and refining is crucial. There is an enormous difference between crude ore and twenty-four-karat gold.

Now, pay attention to this. The mind also needs to be purified in order to recover its own luster. To win the grace of your own mind, you have to *do* something. It is something very important — you must practice austerities. The Sanskrit word for *austerity* is *tapas,* and *tapa*s means "heating, burning." Now, this does not refer to physical torture, nor does it refer to mental torture. It is not something like "no pain, no gain." *Tapas* refers to something very different.

What austerities, what *tapas,* can you perform to win the grace of the mind? How can you truly purify the mind? What tools do you need to discover your golden mind? What will make a golden mind possible?

The answer can be found in the *Bhagavad-Gītā.* Listen carefully. These words carry our golden guidance for the brilliant year of 1999. In the *Bhagavad-Gītā* Lord Kṛṣṇa tells us:

> *manaḥ-prasādaḥ sāumyatvaṁ māunam ātma-vinigrahaḥ*
> *bhāva-saṁśuddhir ity etat tapo mānasam ucyate*
>
> Peace of mind, gentleness, silence, self-restraint, and purity of being: these are called austerities of the mind.[6]

What luminous, golden nuggets of wisdom. Today we will look at them very briefly. Then we will have the rest of the year to study them more closely, so that our minds and our lives may become as golden as a field in the first rays of morning.

The first austerity of the mind is *manaḥ-prasāda,* peace of mind, tranquility of the mind. Or, as Bābā says, "the grace of the mind." The grace of the mind is possible only if you are able to fully understand what it means to make peace with God. Lord Kṛṣṇa says, "I am the mind." What an exalted awareness to have. Within your own mind, God exists. It is awesome: within your own mind, the supreme light exists. So by making peace with your own mind, you are actually establishing an unshakable relationship with the supreme Benefactor. You are making peace with God.

Everyone seems to understand that before you die, you have to make your peace with God. However, in the yogic tradition, you do not wait till your last rites. You make peace with your own mind on a daily basis. Yoga understands the power that the mind has over you. It is your mind that decides whether or not to follow your resolutions. It chooses whether or not to listen to others. It exercises its options all the time. It opts to bamboozle you or to seek the light. The mind is extremely powerful. It can sway you to such an extent, to such an extreme, that any return seems impossible. Haven't you heard people say, "He is a goner"? Therefore, you have to make peace with your own mind. Now, my dear ones. Listen. I mean *now*. Can you hear me? Now.

A mind of gold creates a golden life. A golden mind sustains a golden life. There are many great techniques to bring serenity to the mind. It is good to experiment with them and find what works best for you. See when and how your mind is able to become calm. Learn to recreate that environment. Learn to expand the calm state of consciousness. Learn to carry that experience into your day-to-day activities.

For example, everything in nature can evoke peace of mind. It is very helpful to focus the mind on the vast blue sky, a beautiful stream, a golden sunrise. We are talking about *manaḥ-prasāda* — tranquility of the mind, calmness of the mind, serenity of the mind, the grace of the mind. And we are looking at some of the tools, some of the techniques, to bring serenity to the mind. Listening to wise counsel can make you peaceful. Another person's wisdom can expand the tranquility of your mind. All the spiritual disciplines — such as meditation, chanting the mantra, contemplation — can be considered austerities of the mind.

Bābā used to take great delight in telling everyone that these spiritual disciplines were not for attaining God, because God is already attained. The practices exist just to purify the mind. For example, when you chant the mantra, you soon notice that your mind is becoming calmer. When tranquility of mind spreads through your being, you also experience a very deep connection to the Truth, to your deepest love, to your own God within. And with this comes bliss beyond measure. *Manaḥ-prasāda,* an austerity that leads to bliss.

In the beginning, I said this is an initiation. As you sit with the Message and contemplate its different aspects, we will also be practicing what we are speaking about. Right now, we will chant the mantra *Oṁ,* the primordial sound. Let the sound spread tranquility throughout your being. *Oṁ.*[7] *A golden mind, a golden life.*

Now, my beloved ones, let us hear the second golden nugget of wisdom that Lord Kṛṣṇa gives us. It is gentleness, *saumya.* We just discussed *manaḥ-prasāda,* the tranquility of the mind. The second golden nugget of wisdom is *saumya,* gentleness.

You may be wondering why Lord Kṛṣṇa gives gentleness such a high place and why it is considered an austerity. Well, consider the opposite of gentleness. It is terribly unappealing. An irritable mind — what a miserable way to live. It is said that the physical body can actually develop a condition called irritable bowel syndrome. That irritation is enough to ruin your health completely. Slowly but surely, every system in the body begins to decline. Think of this now. With an irritable mind your whole life declines.

Your mind affects every aspect and facet of your life. Sleep is no escape from the mind. Even your dreams filter through it. Therefore, familiarize yourself with this austerity, *saumya,* gentleness, to rid the mind of its tendency to bristle. Just imagine a person suddenly striding up to you, abruptly thrusting out his hand and grabbing your arm for no reason. What do you feel? What is your reaction? How much time do you want to spend with that person?

Now think of your own mind. What are the consequences to your body and your soul when your mind is harsh, abrupt, ruthless, rude, snarling, inflexible, and insensitive? What is the state of your being? How can you live with something like that inside of you? How can you relax enough even to draw breath? Therefore, the scriptures advise you to purify the mind in the fire of austerity to bring about gentleness.

It is well known that gold is the softest of all metals. It is also the least reactive. For instance, gold never reacts with oxygen, which means it will not rust or tarnish. In every environment where it is found, whether natural or industrial, gold is benign. In the same way, do you realize that your mind has a natural capacity for gentleness? It is a great practice to nurture this quality without letting the mind lose its strength and elasticity. *Saumya,* gentleness.

One of the ways to follow the austerity of gentleness is by cultivating *viveka,* discrimination, the power to discern. The *Kaṭha Upaniṣad* talks about *śreyas* and *preyas,* the beneficial and the pleasurable. It says:

śreyaś ca preyaś ca manuṣyam etas
tau samparītya vivinakti dhīraḥ
śreyo hi dhīro'bhi preyaso vṛṇīte
preyo mando yoga-kṣemād vṛṇīte

> Both the beneficial and the pleasurable present themselves to a human being. The wise person assesses them, notes the difference, and chooses the beneficial over the pleasurable. But the unwise person chooses the pleasurable rather than what is beneficial.[8]

Viveka, yogic discrimination, is the ability to perceive what will be beneficial in the long run. It is not always so obvious. This discrimination, this steady wisdom, lays a very good foundation on which to build strength of mind. When your mind immediately falls prey to that which is merely gratifying, when your mind gets attracted only to that which is gratifying and ignores the consequences, it loses the power of gentleness. However, when the mind is able to tell the difference between *śreyas* and *preyas,* it becomes free from greed, anger, envy, and so on. The more *viveka,* the more discrimination you acquire, the more your mind softens and opens.

Have you ever noticed that in tales and legends there is often an elderly person who is very wise and temperate? Such elders are always depicted as being gentle, even when others do wrong. Why? These elders perceive that gentleness is more beneficial than severity in helping others to grow and improve. They practice *viveka,* discrimination.

What else encourages gentleness? When your mind is focused on the Lord who dwells within the mind, you experience great humility. Humility brings about gentleness. This is why when you first receive *śaktipāt,* you are awed at the immensity of the experience. You say, "In my being, God is present. God is alive in my life." You experience great humility and, therefore, great gentleness envelops you.

The mind also acquires the texture of gentleness by constantly contemplating God's infinite mercy. How many times do you find yourself thanking God? Sometimes while you are thinking about God and understanding the gratitude you are experiencing, you say, "Thank God!" At other times when something goes wrong, you say, "Oh, God!" Then all of a sudden there's a miracle, and you say, "Thank God, thank God!" How many times have you whispered, "Thank God, thank God, thank God," when you're by yourself, when you're out in public, walking down the road, flying in a plane, reading about someone's death. "Thank God, thank God." God's infinite mercy. Such beautiful words: *infinite mercy.*

In its natural state, the mind relishes gentleness. Therefore, I invite you to this daily practice of gentleness in this happy 1999. *Saumya*: make it a daily austerity to practice gentleness in its true golden form.

Once again let us chant the syllable *Oṁ*. Let your entire being fill with gentleness. *Oṁ. A golden mind, a golden life.*

Now, my sweet ones, listen to the third golden nugget of wisdom. Can you hear it? *Maunam.* Silence. You must be wondering, in this age of information, what silence? Who has time to think about silence when you are so busy getting information from one end of the world to the other?

Communication — that is the mantra of this modern age, *kali-yuga.* Without communication, people feel like fish out of water. "No e-mail? No fax? Nobody called? No letters? Oh, no! I better see what's happening." And you send thirty e-mails to thirty different people; and then within half an hour dozens of messages come back. "Ahh, ahh! They love me." In olden days they used to say, "No news is good news." But now . . .

They say the globe is getting smaller and smaller. Every day it is getting smaller. The sheer volume of communication has eliminated distance, as you know, and collapsed our sense of space. On one hand, all this dialogue has produced a kind of togetherness in this world. We feel we are one. Everybody gets to know everything right away. That's nice, isn't it? You get to know what your daughter is doing, what your son is doing, what your grandfather is doing, and what your uncle did. You find out everything. However, it has also sabotaged serenity. Silence, precious silence, has been drowned out by a cacophony of voices. And this is a calamity for humankind. When we get sick, why can't we get better as quickly as our forefathers and foremothers did? There is no silence. When your body is ailing, it needs quietude. When your mind is suffering, it needs quietude. Silence, precious silence.

For a golden mind, silence is absolutely essential. Silence is practiced in every single spiritual tradition in this world. There are two main ways to establish silence. One is to give your tongue a rest, to curb its incessant activity. As a saying goes, the tongue weighs practically nothing, but so few people can hold it.

The other way to attain silence is to let the mind come to rest, to quiet its activity, to let its thoughts cease. "Silence is golden"— we have all heard that. Every evening when the golden sun sets, you can actually feel silence spreading, you can feel silence descending. An atmosphere of stillness, a hush, spreads over the earth. Even when the night creatures come out of their holes and caves and bushes to prowl around, even if the coyotes and wolves howl and the crickets and the cicadas make their noises, the silence is present. It is so present, you can almost touch it. You can almost drink it.

This silence is vital. Even the energy of nature must be replenished. Therefore, there is so much silence in nature. They say in outer space there is hardly any noise. There is no gravity; there is no noise. Total silence. Silence is the most natural thing in the world, it is the most natural thing in this universe. Imagine in the olden days, going home after a good day of work in the field. Silence is the path you take back. Silence is what comes with you to your dwelling, your sacred dwelling, your own Heart. Although silence is present, it can bear fruit only if you know how to observe it, to invoke it, to practice it.

There are different ways to practice *maunam*, silence. For example, suppose someone is talking and you feel the urge to interrupt, even though you know it is not going to be beneficial. Hold your tongue in check. Start from there. Keep silence. Or suppose you find yourself disagreeing with someone. Suppose the person is making a very strong statement and you strenuously disagree. You disapprove completely. You are uncomfortable and you want to contradict them. You want to humiliate them. Check the impulse. Hold your tongue. Observe silence. Speak when it is your turn. Make your point; it will be well taken.

Bābā says:

> The power and the effectiveness of your words increase in direct proportion to the silence that you observe.[9]

That statement has all the power of Bābā's silence, his own *sādhanā*. It is a kind of silence that can only be gained through spiritual practices. It is so deep. You walked into Bābā's presence, you entered his energy field — silence, deep silence, would descend upon you. It would spread throughout your being.

How do you go about observing silence on all levels, from the gross to the subtle? The best aid is the mantra. The best example is the mantra. You repeat the mantra with your tongue first, then the vibrations of the mantra descend into the throat. You do not even have to repeat the mantra with your tongue anymore. You can feel the vibrations of the mantra in the throat region. And then as you continue to practice the mantra, the vibrations of the mantra descend into the heart. You can hear the mantra in the heart. Let me tell you, it is the sweetest moment, it is truly paradise when you hear the sound of your own heart. It is the most melodious sound you can ever, ever, ever hear in this universe. This is why you should know your heart is golden. Your heart is very sweet.

You feel the vibrations of the mantra in the heart region, and then they descend into the navel region. There you feel the mantra — pulsing, pulsing, and pulsing. When that happens, you experience an unearthly silence in your whole being. You rest. You truly rest. *Maunam.* The mantra purifies the tongue, the throat, the heart, and you feel it arising from the deepest part of your being. As purification takes place, as you become increasingly aware of the power of the mantra vibrating at subtle levels, you experience silence.

You can actually see silence in a leaf, in a rock, in a person, in an object. What you see is silence pulsating. It draws you deep inside yourself, the purification. This practice of going within will take you even deeper into the world of silence where everything sparkles, sparkles, sparkles.

Now as we chant *Oṁ,* allow it to transport you to the golden silence of your mind. *Oṁ. A golden mind, a golden life.*

Bābā's words, and the words of all the scriptures, are so precious, so strong, so powerful. So friendly, too. You want to embrace their advice. The fourth golden nugget of wisdom that Lord Kṛṣṇa gives us in chapter 17 of the *Bhagavad-Gītā* is self-restraint, *ātma-vinigraha.* Some of the other words that are used to define this great austerity are *self-control, self-discipline, control of the senses, subjugating the mind, taming the mind, tightening the reins of the mind,* and *stilling the modifications of the mind.* When you hear about this austerity, please don't squirm. There is no reason to feel concerned. Don't be troubled, please. And I want to ask you a favor. Don't think, "This is not for me — self-restraint." Don't close your ears and shut your mind to this golden nugget of Lord Kṛṣṇa's wisdom. Open yourself up and pay attention to this extraordinary expression of the meaning of self-restraint.

Bābā Muktānanda says:

> We should understand why restraint of the senses is emphasized. The seers were not interested in tormenting people, and they were not antagonistic toward the senses as such. They did not hold the senses responsible for anything. They recommended self-control only so

> that we can collect the energy of the spirit. The vibrations of that energy are pouring out through the senses and getting scattered in the external world. If we collect this energy and turn it back toward itself, we experience the great Self.[10]

Collecting the energy of the spirit: self-restraint. This is the beginning of the golden year 1999. Now, in your own way, you must have already made many, many resolutions. Perhaps, like some people, you were a little disheartened at the end of 1998 — disappointed in yourself because you could not carry out your resolutions or you could not really maintain your most cherished resolution. You could not fulfill the promise to yourself. You did not overcome, for example, your greatest fault — like biting your nails or some such habit — or you did not realize your dearest dream. And so maybe you find the very thought of making more resolutions exhausting.

If that is the case, wouldn't you like to try a little bit of this sacred formula? Experience the tranquility of the mind, the true gentleness of your mind, the supreme silence of your own mind, and allow yourself to become the master of your senses.

Self-restraint, as Bābā said, is not about tormenting yourself. Subjugating the mind does not mean tearing it to shreds and hanging it out to dry. It is not some kind of ancient form of torture. Self-restraint means self-inquiry. It means living consciously.

When you see a little baby reaching out to touch a fire, what do you do? You pull her back, you keep her from hurting herself. When you are horseback riding, it is natural, it is instinctive, to keep your horse from galloping along the edge of a cliff. If you go swimming in the ocean, you are constantly trying to avoid the undercurrent. While a plant is growing, you protect it so it won't be trampled by people or gobbled up by small animals. If you have a *pūjā*, a space that is dedicated to supreme worship, you maintain its sanctity. You keep it clean. You keep it pure. Why? Because it is natural to take care of what matters to you. With *ātma-vinigraha*, self-restraint, that is exactly what you do with your golden life. You are taking care of something that matters to you. It is your golden life. It is a present from God.

This year, 1999, is a present from time. We made a resolution. We said, "Let us embrace it as a present from time, from God." And therefore, it matters to you. Self-restraint simply means being watchful. Practicing vigilance is not being hurtful to your senses. Yes, ascetics in the past performed severe austerities to mortify their flesh. They tried to separate themselves from body-consciousness in order to attain immortal bliss. Yes, they abstained from anything with even a remote hint of sensuality. Yes, they did torture their bodies with intense forms of deprivation because they believed that is how they would enter the kingdom of God. However, in the Siddha Yoga philosophy, this sort of thing is not recommended. It may have been all right for some yogis or ascetics or saints, but it is not the medicine for everyone.

Siddha Yoga philosophy takes the path of moderation, and that is exactly what we mean by self-restraint, *ātma-vinigraha.* And this is what self-restraint glorifies: moderation, fine balance. It is just as Bābā explains so clearly and beautifully: The vibrations of the energy of the spirit pour out through the senses. You do not want to dissipate this energy. This energy is so precious that you want to gather it. You want to accumulate *śakti-puñja,* a mass of divine energy, because it has the power to uplift you. It can bring you into the presence of God. It can make your life golden, a mass of divine energy. You can amass a mass of divine energy through self-restraint.

How do you gather this energy? You can practice self-control in many ways: in your manner of speaking, your way of thinking, your manner of listening, your way of tasting and seeing. In all the different activities of the senses, you can observe self-control. But remember, moderation is the golden key. Any time you go too far, you know it. Eventually, instead of being stuck with 20/20 hindsight, you come to trust your own intuition, your own early-warning system, to keep you on track. By practicing self-restraint, you learn to be watchful, or mindful. This practice actually becomes second nature.

Then it does not feel like a severe austerity. It becomes a part of your life, and you come to love it.

Now, once again, let us chant *Oṁ*. Let the sound of *Oṁ* draw the energy of the senses into the heart. *Oṁ. A golden mind, a golden life.*

Doesn't this golden 1999 feel pure? Isn't that the case with anything that is new and fresh? Doesn't your heart get drawn to the pure essence of everything, whatever it may be? There is something alluring about purity.

We have one more brilliant nugget of wisdom to explore from this verse from the *Bhagavad-Gītā*. The fifth golden nugget of wisdom that Lord Kṛṣṇa names is *bhāva-saṁśuddhi*, purity of being. This austerity covers almost everything on the spiritual path that leads a seeker to the experience of a golden mind and a golden life. *Bhāva-saṁśuddhi*, purity of being. To capture the essence of the Sanskrit, there are many translations of *bhāva-saṁśuddhi*: purity of heart, purity of spirit, the cleansing of one's affections, the honesty of one's motives, purity of nature.

So you see, *bhāva-saṁśuddhi* cannot just be defined as "purity of being" but as the whole interior of your consciousness. It is everything that you are, from inside out, from outside in. *Bhāva-saṁśuddhi* must take place in every aspect of your state:

your thoughts, your feelings, your motives, your desires, your attitudes. It's a vast territory, isn't it?

This is why we emphasize the necessity of ongoing contemplation, bringing all the dark corners of your psyche into your conscious awareness so that you can offer them up to the fire of Consciousness. The only reason you would dig them up is so that you can offer them back to the fire of Consciousness, and you can experience *bhāva-saṁśuddhi,* purity of being.

Why is purity of being so essential? Until you realize your own golden nature, your mind is driven by a desire for what the scriptures call ephemeral, impermanent things, and it wanders far away from the effervescent experience of the supreme Self. Therefore, you must keep tabs on what is happening inside you. For example, on the outside, when dirty clothes pile up, what do you do? You wash them. You have to do the laundry.

Now, what about your mind when negative thoughts accumulate — gloomy, hopeless, anxious, guilty, blaming thoughts? When your mind accumulates these so-called unwanted things, what do you do? Do you say, "Well! That is just me. That is how I am. My mother told me even when I was four years old, I was like that. Take it or leave it. It's just me." Do you say, "Well, that is my mind. What to do? It's the way my mind is." No, drop it. That is not you. That is just not you.

The scriptures say you are Śiva, you are the supreme Self, you are pure, you are Consciousness. The sages sing your praises:

"You are great. You are beautiful. You are the best. You are pure. You are Consciousness. You are Śiva. You are Śiva. You are Śiva."

Then why do you hold on to your negative thoughts? They are not you. They are not you *at all.* Remember, you must follow the advice of the sages. Here we are, walking on this golden path, at this golden time, in this golden company, to receive the golden fruit. So, let go of those negative thoughts. *Bhāva-saṁśuddhi,* purity of being.

How can you let go of them? Can you just say, "Oh, Gurumayi said, 'Drop it'"? Well, you *could* . . . However, if for some reason you *can't* . . . This is why we perform austerities. Remember the sweet word *austerity*? This is why we perform austerities.

Bhāva-saṁśuddhi, purity of being, is a determining factor in the success of your efforts to Self-realization. First, you restrain the senses from impure objects. Then, you can cultivate purity of being by giving the senses pure objects: objects that will bring about beneficial results, that will uplift your consciousness, bring you to God, and make your life golden. The Siddha Yoga practices do confer purity of being very easily.

The schedule in Siddha Yoga retreats has been designed to refocus your attention to reach for that which is beneficial, that which is essential. When Bābā traveled around the world, he took the *āśram* schedule with him. The Siddha Yoga retreats reflect this schedule. In these retreats powerful austerities take place. They create a fire of purification in your being. All the impurities, the thoughts and habits that cloud your mind, burn away like dross from gold.

A little while ago, we used the image of gold being refined in the craftsman's fire. The Siddha Yoga practices work in the same way. The grace and purity within them are great. They ignite the inner fire that refines and purifies the mind until, like gold, its true radiance, its natural brilliance, is released. *A golden mind, a golden life.* The fire of yoga is like a great *yajña,* the fire ritual that brāhmin priests in India have been performing for thousands of years. Just as the brāhmins make offerings to the fire — the purest oils, the purest grains, the purest hymns of praise, and the purest intentions — in the same way, you nourish the inner fire with the practices of Siddha Yoga.

When you chant many, many rounds of the *Guru-Gītā,* you are creating the fire of *svādhyāya.* When you chant the mantra in a sustained way for a long time, you are creating the fire of the mantra that spreads throughout your being. When you focus on the breathing process, you are creating the fire of *prāṇa,* the breath, the breath of fire. When you sit for many hours in meditation, you are creating the fire of meditation. By performing each austerity, you are a priest of your own *yajña.*

Purity of being gives rise to the natural innocence of a newborn baby. It makes your heart overflow with gratitude for your golden life. You are able to perceive the entire universe bathed in perpetual freshness, in the soft splendor of the early morning light. *Oṁ.* The purity of being. *Oṁ.*

Once again let us chant *Oṁ. Una mente de oro, una vida de oro. A golden mind, a golden life. Svarṇim man, svarṇim jīvan.*

We have completed the five austerities that Lord Kṛṣṇa describes for a golden mind, a golden life. We have sung the primordial sound *Oṁ.* The purpose of all these austerities is to prepare you for Self-realization. Their fruit is the *darśan* of God. Their fruit is the experience of the inner Self. When the mind has been completely purified, it becomes golden. Then it can reflect the light of the Lord into your entire life. Bābā Muktānanda expresses it so beautifully:

> The earth is holy and filled with God. The breeze that blows is holy and filled with God. Fire that burns is holy and filled with God. These are the kinds of thoughts you must be thinking all the time.[11]

A golden mind, a golden life. Let us walk together on this golden path, through this golden year, in this golden company, always knowing it is a golden time to receive the golden fruit. We will be experiencing and relishing the golden fruit throughout the year.

Tranquility of the mind, gentleness of the mind, silence of the mind, self-restraint of the senses, purity of being. Bābā is with you. Grace is with you. And we are together. A golden life, a golden mind. *A golden mind, a golden life.*

With great respect, with great love, I welcome you all with all my heart.

Sadgurunāth Mahārāj kī Jay!

GUIDE TO SANSKRIT PRONUNCIATION

In Sanskrit every letter is pronounced; there are no silent letters. Every letter has only one sound, except for the letter **v** (see below).

LENGTH OF VOWELS

Vowels are either short or long. Short vowels are **a**, **i** and **u**. Long vowels are **ā**, **ī**, **ū**, **e**, and **o**. A long vowel is held for twice as long as a short one.

VOWELS

The English equivalents are approximations.

a as in *but* or *cup*	**ā** as in *father*
i as in *feet* or *seat*	**ī** as in *scene* or *mean*
u as in *boot*	**ū** as in *pool* or *mood*
e as in *save* or *weigh*	**o** as in *toe*

ṛ is a vowel that sounds like the **ur** in *church* or the **re** in *acre.*

The next two vowels are diphthongs, combinations of sounds that are made up of two distinct vowels pronounced in rapid succession. Each diphthong, represented by two letters in English, is written as a single letter in the Sanskrit alphabet.

ai	is a combination of long **ā** and short **i** sounds, as in *pie* or *sky.*
au	is a combination of long **ā** and short **u**, as in *bough* or *cow.*

CONSONANTS

c	as in *such,* never as in *cave* or *celery.*
t, d, n	are pronounced with the tip of the tongue against the top teeth.
ṭ, ḍ, ṇ	are pronounced with the tip of the tongue bent slightly back to touch the roof of the mouth.
r	is a rolled **r** as in Spanish *para.*
v	is a soft **v** when following a vowel or beginning a word, and is a **w** pronounced with unrounded lips when following a consonant.
ś	as in *shine* or *shower.*

CONSONANTS *(continued)*

ṣ	is pronounced like **ś**, except that the tip of the tongue is bent slightly back toward the roof of the mouth, as in English *assure*.
ñ	as in *onion* or Spanish *señor*; also as in *punch*.
jñ	as **gnya**. Represents a single letter in the Sanskrit alphabet.
ḥ	at the end of a sentence indicates that the previous vowel is echoed; for example, *iḥ* is pronounced *ihi*.

When consonants are followed by **h**, as in **bh** or **dh**, the consonant is aspirated, as in *abhor*.

A consonant written twice, such as **dd** or **tt**, is pronounced as a single sound and is held twice as long as a single consonant.

NOTES

Foreword

1. These Siddha Yoga Message talks were given at the beginning of each new year between 1995 and 2004. Volume I presents the Message talks given for the years 1995–1999. Volume II will present the talks given for 2000–2004.
2. "Approach the Present with Your Heart's Consent. Make It a Blessed Event," Siddha Yoga Message for the year 2001. To appear in *Sādhanā of the Heart,* vol. 2 (South Fallsburg, NY: SYDA Foundation, forthcoming).
3. Ibid.
4. "Blaze the Trail of Equipoise and Enter the Heart, the Divine Splendor," in *Sādhanā of the Heart,* vol. 1, 20.
5. "Be Filled with Enthusiasm and Sing God's Glory," in *Sādhanā of the Heart,* vol. 1, 26.
6. The nondual Shaivite philosophy of Kashmir, also known as Kashmir Shaivism, encompasses a series of philosophical texts on the spiritual path formulated in the Kashmir region of what is now India from approximately the ninth through the twelfth centuries. This tradition, which refers to the supreme Reality as Śiva, is advocated by sages such as Vasugupta, Utpaladeva, and Abhinavagupta, and is one of the fundamental philosophies reflected in the teachings of the Siddha Yoga path.
7. "Approach the Present with Your Heart's Consent. Make It a Blessed Event," to appear in *Sādhanā of the Heart,* vol. 2.

Blaze the Trail of Equipoise and Enter the Heart, the Divine Splendor

January 24, 1995, Shree Muktānanda Ashram, South Fallsburg, New York.

1. Mohandas K. (Mahātmā) Gandhi (1869–1948).
2. Swāmī Muktānanda, from unpublished material.
3. Henry Parry Liddon (1829–1890), British theologian.

4. Swāmī Muktānanda, "Introduction," *The Nectar of Chanting* (South Fallsburg, NY: SYDA Foundation, 1994), x.
5. A. K. Ramanujan, *Speaking of Śiva* (London: Penguin Books Inc., 1973), 164. Reprinted by permission of Penguin Books Ltd.
6. *Uddhava-Gītā,* 2.37
Translation adapted from Swāmī Madhavānanda, *Uddhava Gītā or The Last Message of Shri Kṛṣṇa* (Calcutta: Advaita Ashrama, 1993), 32.
7. Retold from a story by Anthony De Mello, S.J., *Taking Flight: A Book of Story Meditations* (New York: Doubleday Image Books, 1990), 161.

Be Filled with Enthusiasm and Sing God's Glory

January 1, 1996, Palm Springs, California.

1. Swāmī Muktānanda, *Play of Consciousness* (South Fallsburg, NY: SYDA Foundation, 2000), 262.
2. Swāmī Muktānanda, *Satsang with Baba* (Oakland, CA: SYDA Foundation, 1977), vol. 3, 322.
3. This and the subsequent passage in this paragraph are from Mark S. G. Dyczkowski, *The Doctrine of Vibration: An Analysis of the Doctrines and Practices of Kashmir Shaivism* (Albany: State University of New York Press, 1987), 149.
4. Muktānanda, *Satsang with Baba,* vol. 2 (1976), 294.
5. Verse traditionally attributed to the *Rāmāyaṇa.*
6. Swāmī Muktānanda, *From the Finite to the Infinite* (South Fallsburg, NY: SYDA Foundation, 1994), 3.

Wake Up to Your Inner Courage and Become Steeped in Divine Contentment

January 1, 1997, Shree Muktānanda Ashram, South Fallsburg, New York.

1. *Bhagavad-Gītā* 11.40
English translation adapted from Winthrop Sargeant, *Shrī Bhagavad Gītā* (Albany: State University of New York Press, 1993), 181-182.
2. *Kulārṇava Tantra* 9.37
English translation adapted from M. P. Pandit, *Gems from the Tantras* (Pondicherry: All India Press, 1975), 38.

3. Daniel Ladinsky, *I Heard God Laughing: Renderings of Hafiz* (Walnut Creek, CA: Sufism Reoriented, 1996), 45.
4. Swāmī Muktānanda, "Cultivate the Self," *Siddha Path* (December 1981): 13.
5. John Balguy (1686–1748), British theologian.
6. Akka Mahādevī. *Darshan: In the Company of the Saints* 95 (February 1995): 27. Original source unknown.
7. Swāmī Muktānanda, *Sadgurunath Maharaj ki Jay* (New York, 1975), 107.
8. Swāmī Muktānanda, *Conversations with Swami Muktananda* (South Fallsburg, NY: SYDA Foundation, 1998), 230.
9. *Ham Dīvāno, bhajan* (devotional song) in the Hindi language. Newly translated for this talk. Original source in oral tradition.

Refresh Your Resolution. Smile at Your Destiny.

January 1, 1998, Palm Springs, California.

1. "Happy New Year" in Spanish, French, Urdu, and Hindi.
2. *Merā maksad hai tujhī se, qawwali* (Sūfī devotional song) in the Urdu language. Newly translated for this talk. Original source in oral tradition.
3. *Atharva-Veda,* 20.17.6
   Newly translated for this talk.
4. *Ṛg-Veda,* 7.34.5,6
   English translation rendered from Svami Satya Prakash Sarasvati and Satyakam Vidyalankar, *Ṛgveda Saṃhitā* (New Delhi: Veda Pratishthana, 1980), vol. 8, 2457.
5. Swāmī Muktānanda, *I Have Become Alive* (South Fallsburg, NY: SYDA Foundation, 1992), 34.
6. Poem by Jalal al-Din Rumi, newly rendered for this talk.
7. Swāmī Muktānanda, "The World Is As You See It," *Baba Company* 3, no. 2 (Summer 1980): 2.
8. Henry Ward Beecher (1813–1887), American preacher, orator, and writer.
9. Poetic rendering of the *Śrī Sūkta,* verse 4.

10. *Guru-Gītā,* verse 92
    The Nectar of Chanting (South Fallsburg, NY: SYDA Foundation, 1994), 32.

    śvetāmbaraṁ śveta-vilepa-puṣpaṁ
    muktā-vibhūṣam muditam dvi-netram /
    vāmāṅka-pīṭha-sthita-divya-śaktim
    manda-smitaṁ sāndra-kṛpā-nidhānam //

    He [the Guru] has two eyes. He is clad in white garments. He is besmeared with white paste and is adorned with (garlands of) white flowers and pearls. He is joyous. He has a gentle smile. He is a treasure house of abundant grace. The divine Śakti is seated on the left side of his lap.
11. Swāmī Muktānanda, *Bhagawan Nityananda of Ganeshpuri* (South Fallsburg, NY: SYDA Foundation, 1996), 5.
12. Swāmī Muktānanda, *Satsang with Baba* (Oakland, CA: SYDA Foundation, 1978), vol. 5, 192.

A Golden Mind, A Golden Life

January 1, 1999, Santa Clara, California.

1. Translated into Spanish and Hindi.
2. *Ṛg-Veda,* 1.6.3
   Newly translated for this talk.
3. *Kaivalya Upaniṣad,* verse 20
   Rendered from translation by S. Radhakrishnan, *The Principal Upaniṣads* (London: George Allen & Unwin Ltd. and New York: Humanities Press Inc., 1974), 931.
4. *Bhagavad-Gītā* 10.22
   Winthrop Sargeant, *Shrī Bhagavad Gītā* (Albany: State University of New York Press, 1993), 156-157.
5. Swāmī Muktānanda, *Satsang with Baba* (Oakland, CA: SYDA Foundation, 1976), vol. 2, 191.
6. *Bhagavad-Gītā* 17.16
   Sargeant, *Shri Bhagavad Gītā,* 250.
7. This is the first of five chanting sessions of the syllable *Oṁ.* To enhance your contemplation and experience of the talk, you might want to pause and chant *Oṁ* when each of these chanting sessions is introduced.

8. *Kaṭha Upaniṣad,* 2.2
English translation rendered from Patrick Olivelle, *Upaniṣads* (Oxford: Oxford University Press, 1996), 235.
9. Swāmī Muktānanda, *Conversations with Swāmī Muktānanda* (South Fallsburg, NY: SYDA Foundation, 1998), 162.
10. Muktānanda, *Satsang with Baba,* vol. 3 (1977), 49.
11. Muktānanda, *Satsang with Baba,* vol. 1 (1974), 15.

GLOSSARY

All terms are Sanskrit unless otherwise indicated.

ADṚṢṬA

Lit., "unseen." Unseen force of fate or destiny. More specifically, the power of present actions, virtuous and nonvirtuous, to cause later pleasure or pain.

AKKA MAHĀDEVĪ

Twelfth-century poet-saint of South India who composed many devotional poems *(vacanas)* in the Kannada language; a member of the Vīraśaiva movement.

ALLAMA PRABHU

Twelfth-century saint and mystic of South India's Vīraśaiva movement; presided over a large group of saints, who often assembled to share their love of God through teachings, poems, and songs.

ARJUNA

One of the heroes of the Indian epic, the *Mahābhārata*, a great warrior and a disciple of Lord Kṛṣṇa. *See also* BHAGAVAD-GĪTĀ; KṚṢṆA.

ĀŚRAM (Hindi; Sanskrit=*āśrama*)

A place of disciplined retreat, where seekers engage in spiritual practice and study sacred teachings. *See also* GURUDEV SIDDHA PEEṬH.

ATHARVA-VEDA

See VEDA(S).

BĀBĀ (Hindi)

Term of affection and respect for an elderly person, a saint, or a holy man. Swāmī Muktānanda, Gurumayi's Guru, was widely known as Bābā. *See also* MUKTĀNANDA, SWĀMĪ; SIDDHA GURU.

BHAGAVAD-GĪTĀ

One of the world's treasures of spiritual wisdom, the centerpiece of the Indian epic, the *Mahābhārata*. In eighteen chapters, Lord Kṛṣṇa instructs his disciple Arjuna about steady wisdom, meditation, the nature of God, the supreme Self, and spiritual knowledge and practice. *See also* ARJUNA; KṚṢṆA.

BHĀGYA
Fate, destiny, fortune, good fortune, prosperity.

BHAJAN (Hindi)
Devotional song in the Hindi language.

BRAHMIN (Hindi; Sanskrit=*brāhmaṇa*)
Member of a hereditary social class of India. Brahmins are traditionally priests and scholars.

CAMATKĀRA
Astonishment, surprise, poetic charm, expansive wonder inspired by the experience of the Divine.

CONSCIOUSNESS (Sanskrit=*cit, saṁvit*)
The self-aware and supremely independent divine Power that creates, pervades, supports, dissolves, conceals, and reveals the entire universe as a blissful play. *See also* SELF; TRUTH.

DAKṢIṆĀ
A gift or offering; one of the foundational Siddha Yoga practices through which financial resources are offered for the Guru's work.

DARŚAN (Hindi; Sanskrit=*darśana*)
Lit., "seeing, perceiving, knowing." A vision of a saint; seeing God or an image of God; being in the presence of a holy person. Siddha Yoga students understand *darśan* to be a subtle experience that takes place in the heart.

DEVĪ
The feminine embodiment of the divine Power; any goddess or the Great Goddess. *See also* ŚAKTI.

DHĀRAṆĀ
Centering technique or spiritual exercise in which holding a steady inner focus intensifies one's awareness; the goal is to connect with the Heart, the divine Self.

DHARMA

Right action, that which supports and upholds; one's duty, esp. the highest spiritual duty; actions that are ultimately beneficial for all; behavior that is in alignment with the cosmic order, with one's religion or spiritual path, and with one's role in life.

DĪKṢĀ

Lit., "initiation." More specifically, initiation of a disciple by a Guru into the spiritual path. For Siddha Yoga students, *dīkṣā* takes the form of the awakening of a disciple's *kuṇḍalinī* energy by the grace of the Master; this is known as *śaktipāt-dīkṣā*. *See also* KUṆḌALINĪ ŚAKTI; ŚAKTIPĀT.

GANDHI, MOHANDAS (known as Mahātmā or "great soul")

(1869-1948) A leader of modern India who effected lasting social reforms through the practices of nonviolence, civil disobedience, and self-restraint.

GANGES (Sanskrit=Gaṅgā)

The most sacred river of India, revered as a goddess. Bathing in its waters is said to be highly purifying.

GRACE (Sanskrit=*prasāda, anugraha*)

A cosmic function of God that operates by means of the Guru principle (*guru-tattva*). Attracted by a seeker's longing and focused effort, grace manifests in our world and is bestowed in our lives through the agency of the Guru principle. The living Siddha Guru is the embodiment of the grace-bestowing power of God.

GURU

See SIDDHA GURU.

GURUDEV SIDDHA PEEṬH

Lit., "the sacred abode of a Siddha, a Guru who is one with God." The foundational *āśram* of Gurumayi Chidvilāsānanda and the Siddha Yoga path. Located near Gaṇeśpurī village, in Mahārāṣṭra, India. Initially constructed in 1956 for Swāmī Muktānanda at the command of his Guru, Bhagavān Nityānanda, and formed as a public trust in 1962, Gurudev Siddha Peeṭh is also the location of the *samādhi* shrine (final resting place) of Bābā Muktānanda. *See also* ĀŚRAM.

GURU-GĪTĀ

Lit., "song of the Guru." A sacred text consisting of Sanskrit mantras that describe the nature of the Guru, the Guru-disciple relationship, and techniques of meditation on the Guru. Chanting the *Guru-Gītā* is one of the central practices of Siddha Yoga students.

HAFIZ (or Hafez)

(c. 1325-1390) A Persian master, court poet, and professor of religious studies who is said to have attained the highest state through the grace of his master, Attar. Originally known as Shams-ud-din Mohammed, he received the name Hafiz ("memorizer"), which designates one who knows the *Qur'ān* by heart.

HANUMĀN

One of the heroes of the Indian epic, the *Rāmāyaṇa,* Hanumān is a warrior and chieftain of a semidivine mythological race of monkeys devoted to God in the form of Rāma. Son of the Wind, he performs many acts of courage and daring in defense of his Master, Lord Rāma. He is a symbol of perfect devotion, surrender, and courage. *See also* RĀMĀYAṆA.

HEART

See Foreword (pp. x-xii) for discussion of the term *Heart* within the context of Siddha Yoga teachings.

KAIVALYA UPANIṢAD

An Upaniṣad that teaches renunciation and meditation on supreme Śiva as the means to liberation *(kaivalya). See also* ŚIVA; UPANIṢAD(S).

KALI-YUGA

Lit., "the age of discord." The present age *(yuga)*; in traditional Indian cosmology, said to be a dark age in which righteousness and truth have disintegrated, and discord and strife rule the day. The advantage of being born in this age is that devoted spiritual practice bears fruit more quickly in the face of these challenges, and thus God can be experienced more readily by those who make even a little effort to experience the highest Reality.

KARMA

Lit., "action." Any action, physical, verbal, or mental. Also, the fruition of an action arising from desire. Sometimes the effects of such actions are experienced as pleasurable, sometimes as not pleasurable. One's accumulated karmas determine one's current life situation; however, the manner of responding to one's circumstances is governed by the individual's will.

KASHMIR SHAIVISM

Philosophy elaborated in the collective writings of a number of sages from Kashmir for whom the name Śiva denotes the ultimate Reality. These sages, who flourished from the ninth through the twelfth centuries, recognized the entire universe as a manifestation of *śakti* or divine Power. Bābā Muktānanda found his own experience reflected in the writings of these sages and incorporated their teachings into the philosophical framework of the Siddha Yoga path. *See also* ŚAKTI; SHAIVISM; ŚIVA.

KAṬHA UPANIṢAD

Upaniṣad containing the story of Nachiketas, a young boy who, given a boon by Lord Yama, the Lord of Death, asks for knowledge of the Absolute. *See* UPANIṢAD(S).

KṚṢṆA

Lit., "dark one." The eighth incarnation of Lord Viṣṇu (a name for the all-pervasive, supreme Reality, the sustainer of the universe). Called Kṛṣṇa because of the blue-black color of his skin. *See also* BHAGAVAD-GĪTĀ.

KULĀRṆAVA TANTRA

Shaivite treatise from around the fourteenth century on the practice of yoga; describes the nature of the Guru, the requirements of a disciple, and many traditional practices of worship. *See also* SHAIVISM; YOGA.

KUṆḌALINĪ ŚAKTI

Lit., "coiled one." Spiritual energy lying dormant at the base of the spine; when awakened and guided by a Siddha Guru and nourished by the seeker's disciplined effort, this energy brings about spiritual purification and leads to the permanent experience of one's divine nature. Also refers to the goddess Kuṇḍalinī. *See also* ŚAKTIPĀT; SIDDHA GURU.

LAKṢMĪ

Goddess who embodies prosperity, wealth, good fortune, abundance, success, beauty, grace, charm, splendor, auspiciousness. Another name for Lakṣmī is Śrī.

MAṄGALA

Successful accomplishment; that which promotes such accomplishment; happiness, felicity, well-being, and auspiciousness.

MANTRA

Sacred words or divine sounds invested with the power to purify and transform the awareness of the individual who repeats them. A mantra received from an enlightened Master is enlivened by the power of the Master's attainment. *See also* OṀ NAMAḤ ŚIVĀYA.

MASTER

See SIDDHA GURU.

MĀYĀ

Power that veils the true nature of the Self and projects the experience of multiplicity.

MUKTĀNANDA, SWĀMĪ

(1908-1982) A Siddha Guru of the modern age, often referred to as Bābā; the Guru of Gurumayi Chidvilāsānanda. After wandering the length and breadth of India several times, learning a wide range of spiritual practices and philosophies, he received spiritual initiation in 1947 from his Guru, Bhagavān Nityānanda, and attained Self-realization in 1956. Within a few years, Bābā established the Gurudev Siddha Peeṭh *āśram* in Gaṇeśpurī, India. In 1970, he brought the powerful and rare initiation known as *śaktipāt* to the West, setting in motion what he called a "meditation revolution." Swāmī Muktānanda's final resting place (*samādhi* shrine) is located in Gurudev Siddha Peeṭh. *See also* NITYĀNANDA, BHAGAVĀN; ŚAKTIPĀT; SIDDHA GURU; SIDDHA YOGA.

NASEEB (Urdu, originally from Arabic)

Fate, destiny.

NASRUDDIN, SHEIKH (also known as Mullah Nasruddin)

Generally considered a fictional character popular in Turkish and Persian folklore; used as a central figure in stories told by spiritual teachers to illustrate spiritual lessons and the foibles of the human mind.

NECTAR OF CHANTING, THE

Volume of sacred text chants that includes the chants regularly recited by Siddha Yoga students. *See also* GURU-GĪTĀ; SVĀDHYĀYA.

NITYĀNANDA, BHAGAVĀN

(d. 1961) A Siddha Master, and the Guru of Swāmī Muktānanda; also known as Baḍe Bābā ("elder" Bābā). Considered a born Siddha *(janmasiddha)*, he lived his entire life in the highest state of Consciousness. This natural yogi began his life in northwestern Karṇāṭaka, and later settled in Gaṇeśpurī, Mahārāṣṭra, where eventually thousands of devotees came to be in his presence. Bābā Muktānanda started visiting him in the 1930s, and received *śaktipāt* initiation from him in 1947. His *samādhi* shrine, or final resting place, is located in the village of Gaṇeśpurī, near Gurudev Siddha Peeṭh. *See also* ŚAKTIPĀT; SIDDHA GURU.

NIYATI

Destiny, fate, the fixed order of things, fortune (good or bad).

OṀ

Most sacred of all mantras, considered to be the primordial sound of the vibrating cosmos. An embodiment, in the form of sound, of absolute Consciousness; the pulsation of universal Power. *See also* CONSCIOUSNESS; MANTRA.

OṀ NAMAḤ ŚIVĀYA

Initiation mantra of the Siddha Yoga lineage; known as the great redeeming mantra for its power to grant both worldly fulfillment and spiritual realization. *Oṁ* is the primordial sound; *Namaḥ* means reverence or honor; *Śivāya* denotes divine Consciousness, the Lord who dwells within you as you. *See also* MANTRA; OṀ.

PRĀṆA

Life force; vital energy within living things; vital breath; life.

PRĀRABDHA-KARMA

Results of one's past actions, which one is destined to experience in the present lifetime. *Prārabdha-karma* unfolds even after one attains liberation in the body. *See also* KARMA.

PREYAS

That which is pleasurable only in the short term; contrasted with *śreyas*, that which is ultimately beneficial.

PŪJĀ

Worship; sacred ceremony; the acts and attitudes that increase devotion for one's chosen deity. Also, an altar with images of the Guru or deity and sacred objects used in worship.

PUṆYA KARMA

Merit that comes from auspicious, virtuous, pure, and sacred actions. *See also* KARMA.

PURĀṆAS

Lit., "ancient legends." The eighteen sacred books attributed to the sage Vyāsa, containing stories, legends, and hymns about the creation of the universe, the incarnations of God, the teachings of various deities, and the spiritual legacies of ancient sages and kings.

RĀMĀYAṆA

Epic poem of India, attributed to the sage Vālmīki, which recounts the life and exploits of Lord Rāma, an incarnation of God.

RASA

Flavor, sweetness, juice, nectar; sometimes used as a metaphor for the release of true sweetness in the heart.

ṚG-VEDA

See VEDA(S).

RUMI, JALAL AL-DIN

(1207-1273) Ecstatic poet of the Sūfī mystic tradition; founder of the order of whirling dervishes.

SADBHĀGYA

Good fortune, felicity.

SADGURUNĀTH MAHĀRĀJ KĪ JAY (Hindi)

Lit., "Hail the Lord of true Gurus, the great king!" A joyful invocation of the teacher of the highest Truth both in embodied form and residing within each heart. In the Siddha Yoga tradition this phrase is often recited to invoke auspiciousness at the beginning of an action or activity, and to offer gratitude at the end of an action or activity.

SĀDHANĀ

Leading straight to a goal; a means of accomplishing (something); spiritual practice; worship. The *sādhanā* of Siddha Yoga students includes active, disciplined engagement in the foundational Siddha Yoga practices of meditation, chanting, *sevā*, and *dakṣiṇā*, along with focused study and contemplation of the Siddha Yoga teachings.

ŚAKTI

Lit., "power, energy, strength, capacity." The power of the divine Absolute, often personified as the Great Goddess. *Śakti* is the power that animates and sustains all forms of creation. The term can also refer to a specific power or energy; for example, a power embodied in a particular goddess.

ŚAKTIPĀT (Hindi; Sanskrit=*śaktipāta*)

Lit., "descent of power, descent of grace." In Siddha Yoga, the initiation *(dīkṣā)* by which a Siddha Guru transmits the divine grace that awakens *kuṇḍalinī śakti*, the inner spiritual energy in an aspirant; *śaktipāt dīkṣā* signals the beginning of the *sādhanā* that culminates in spiritual liberation. *See also* KUṆḌALINĪ ŚAKTI; SĀDHANĀ; SIDDHA GURU.

ŚAKTI-PUÑJA

A mass of spiritual energy.

SAṀSĀRA (from the Sanskrit root meaning "revolve")

The cycle of birth, suffering, death, and rebirth that characterizes the existence of a bound soul; also, the mundane world in which that existence is carried out.

SANSKRIT (Sanskrit=*saṁskṛta*)

Lit., "refined, polished, perfected, ornamented." Ancient language of India, considered to be *devavāṇī*, the language of the gods. Sanskrit is the source language for most of the chants, recited texts, and foundational scriptures of the Siddha Yoga path.

SANTOṢA

Satisfaction, contentment.

SATSAṄG (Hindi; Sanskrit=*satsaṅga*)

Lit., "the company of the good." A gathering of seekers for the purpose of meditation, chanting, listening to scriptural teachings, and discussing spiritual topics; an opportunity for spiritual practice.

SAUBHĀGYA

Great good fortune; more specifically, the good fortune of experiencing devotion and becoming aware of grace.

SELF (Sanskrit=*ātman*)

The pure Consciousness that is both the divine core of a human being and the essential nature of all things. *See also* CONSCIOUSNESS; TRUTH.

SEVĀ

Lit., "service, honoring, worship." In Siddha Yoga contexts, selfless service: work offered to God and the Guru, performed as a pure offering, without attachment to the results of one's actions and without desire for personal gain. The English word *sevite* refers to one who practices *sevā*.

SHAIVISM

Term encompassing all the Indian religious and philosophical traditions that take Śiva to be the name for the ultimate Reality. In Siddha Yoga, the term *Shaivism* is generally used to refer to nondual Kashmir Shaivism. *See also* KASHMIR SHAIVISM; ŚIVA.

SHREE MUKTĀNANDA ASHRAM

Siddha Yoga *āśram* in the Catskill Mountains of New York, founded by Swāmī Muktānanda in 1979. *See also* ĀŚRAM.

SIDDHA

Perfected, fully accomplished, Self-realized yogi.

SIDDHA GURU

Perfected spiritual Master who has realized his or her oneness with God, who is able both to bestow *śaktipāt* and guide seekers to spiritual liberation. Such a Guru is also required to be learned in the scriptures and to belong to a lineage of Masters. Another word for Siddha Guru is *sadguru* (lit., "true Guru"). *See also* MUKTĀNANDA, SWĀMĪ; NITYĀNANDA, BHAGAVĀN; ŚAKTIPĀT.

SIDDHA YOGA

The spiritual path taught by Gurumayi Chidvilāsānanda and her Guru, Swāmī Muktānanda. Students of Siddha Yoga engage in practices and apply the teachings shown by the Siddha Guru. The journey of the Siddha Yoga path begins with *śaktipāt dīkṣā* (spiritual initiation). Through the grace of the Siddha Yoga Master and the student's own steady disciplined effort, the journey culminates in the constant recognition of divinity within oneself and within the world. *See also* SĀDHANĀ; ŚAKTIPĀT; SIDDHA GURU.

ŚIVA

In nondual Shaivism, the transcendent and immanent, all-pervasive supreme Reality, the one source of all existence. Also, absolute Reality personified as the deity Lord Śiva. *See also* SHAIVISM.

ŚREYAS

See PREYAS.

ŚRĪ SŪKTA

Three-thousand-year-old hymn, appended to the *Ṛg-Veda*, invoking the goddess Śrī or Lakṣmī. *See also* LAKṢMĪ; VEDA(S).

ŚRĪMAD BHĀGAVATAM

One of the major *Purāṇas*, also known as the *Bhāgavata Purāṇa*, consisting of legends of the various incarnations of Lord Viṣṇu, the sustainer of the universe. *See also* PURĀṆAS.

SŪFĪ

Practitioner of Sufism, the mystical tradition of Islam characterized by ecstatic devotion to God.

SVĀDHYĀYA

Regular, disciplined practice of chanting and recitation of sacred texts in Sanskrit; the process of gaining insight into the nature of the Self through this practice. *See also* GURU-GĪTĀ; NECTAR OF CHANTING, THE.

TAPAS

Lit., "heating." Yogic austerities and disciplined practice (which generate inner heat or "yogic fire") performed to purify both mind and body of any residue of past experience that obscures the direct experience of God; any focused effort in *sādhanā*.

TAPASYA
See TAPAS.

TṚPTI
Satisfaction, contentment.

TRUTH (Sanskrit=*satya, tattva, paramārtha*)
The highest Reality, the awareness that the universe of multiplicity and diversity arises from and is a manifestation of one divine energy. *See also* CONSCIOUSNESS; SELF.

UDDHAVA-GĪTĀ
Section of the *Śrīmad Bhāgavatam,* a scripture composed around the ninth century, in which Lord Kṛṣṇa, on the eve of his departure from the world, gives his final instructions to his beloved disciple Uddhava. *See also* KṚṢṆA; ŚRĪMAD BHĀGAVATAM.

UPANIṢAD(S)
Lit., "sitting down near (a teacher)" or "hidden connection." Concluding portion of the Vedas and the basis for Vedantic philosophy. The various scriptures that constitute the Upaniṣads illuminate the essential teaching that the individual soul and God are one. *See also* VEDA(S).

UTPALADEVA
Tenth-century philosopher, theologian, and poet; one of the foremost sages of nondual Kashmir Shaivism. *See also* KASHMIR SHAIVISM.

VEDA(S)
Lit., "knowledge." The earliest scriptural texts of ancient India, the four Vedas are regarded as divinely revealed, eternal wisdom. The Vedas are, in order of antiquity, *Ṛg-Veda* ("Knowledge of the Hymns"), *Yajur-Veda* ("Knowledge of the Sacrificial Formulas"), *Sāma-Veda* ("Knowledge of the Songs of Praise"), and *Atharva-Veda* ("The Knowledge of [Sage] Atharvan").

VĪRYA
Courage, valor, heroism, vigor, strength, virility, potency, splendor; the vital energy of living creatures.

VIVEKA

Lit., "discernment, discrimination." The faculty that enables a human being to distinguish between reality and illusion, between what is to be cultivated and what discarded on the spiritual path.

YAJÑA

Ancient fire ritual in which oblations are offered to the fire, while sacred mantras are chanted to honor the divine powers of the universe.

YOGA

Lit., "spiritual method, exertion, discipline, (means to) union." A set of disciplined practices utilizing the body, subtle body, and mind. The ultimate goal of yoga is to attain the constant experience of the awareness of the divine Self.

YOGI (masc.; *yoginī*=fem.)

One who practices yoga. *See also* YOGA.

INDEX

FURTHER READING
PUBLISHED BY SYDA FOUNDATION

Selected Books by
Gurumayi Chidvilāsānanda

Collections of Talks

These volumes consist of talks that Gurumayi gave in public programs during teaching retreats. They are essential source material for ongoing contemplation and exploration of the teachings of the Siddha Yoga path.

THE YOGA OF DISCIPLINE

The reader learns how to cultivate yogic discipline and how to apply it creatively to everyday activities. Chapters include discussions of discipline in seeing, listening, eating, speaking, and thinking.

COURAGE AND CONTENTMENT

Opening with Gurumayi's Siddha Yoga Message for 1997, *Wake Up to Your Inner Courage and Become Steeped in Divine Contentment,* this volume expands on the mysterious connection between spiritual courage and true contentment. An invaluable resource for deeper study of this Message.

ENTHUSIASM

This volume includes the talks that Gurumayi gave as she elaborated on the Siddha Yoga Message for 1996, *Be Filled with Enthusiasm and Sing God's Glory.* Those who cultivate the discerning enthusiasm that Gurumayi describes invite its radiance to shine through every action, every thought, every minute of their lives.

MY LORD LOVES A PURE HEART:
The Yoga of Divine Virtues

An extended commentary on chapter 16 of the *Bhagavad-Gītā,* this volume offers clear and precise guidance on how to manifest the magnificent virtues of fearlessness, purity of being, steadfastness, freedom from anger, respect, compassion, humility, and selfless service.

REMEMBRANCE

Through the steady practice of remembrance — remembering our innate goodness, our worthiness to give and receive love, and the extraordinary blessings that flow through our lives — we can attain *mokṣa,* liberation. This is the teaching of *Remembrance.*

INNER TREASURES

The treasure to be discovered here is that joy, peace, and love are not outer qualities to be acquired, but rather reflections of our inner spirit. Turning toward the Heart again and again is the key to making this teaching an everyday reality.

Poetry and Contemplation

PULSATION OF LOVE

In this priceless collection of poetry, Gurumayi generously shares her own experience of discipleship. Through her example we see how faith and perseverance on the path of *gurubhakti* (devotion for the Guru) lead to the attainment of the highest spiritual goal.

SMILE, SMILE, SMILE!

Through poetry Gurumayi expands on the Siddha Yoga Message for 1998, *Refresh Your Resolution. Smile at Your Destiny.* Engaging with these poems, one gains deeper awareness of the process of spiritual contemplation and the perfection of the soul.

THE MAGIC OF THE HEART:
Reflections on Divine Love

"In the supreme Heart the Lord reveals Himself every second of the day." How does one come to live in this experience? Practical and subtle insights are gained from contemplating Gurumayi's tender reflections on divine love.

RESONATE WITH STILLNESS

In a structure designed for daily study, these passages from the writings of Gurumayi and her Guru, Swāmī Muktānanda, support an ongoing practice of focused contemplation.

Picture Books for Young Children

GOOD NIGHT, SWEET DREAMS, I LOVE YOU!

Gurumayi speaks directly to children about love: Love is within you and all around you. Your life is precious, and you are important because of the love in your heart. By remembering and sharing your love with others, you will always stay close to God. An exquisite collage of images complements Gurumayi's teachings.

THE GREAT HISS

From this retelling of a classic Indian fable about an arrogant snake who transforms from town bully into practitioner of astute nonviolence, young people learn that gentleness has a strength and integrity all its own, and that gentleness has the capacity to create harmony in the world.

THE FROGS AND THEIR MONSTER

With the help of a wise friend, a community of frogs overcomes restlessness and fear and wins the prizes of courage and contentment.

Selected Books by
Swāmī Muktānanda

Gurumayi's Guru, Swāmī Muktānanda, widely known as Bābā, wrote many books explaining the philosophy and practices of the Siddha Yoga path.

PLAY OF CONSCIOUSNESS

A rare opportunity to study a first-hand account of the journey to Self-realization. This vital spiritual autobiography by Swāmī Muktānanda describes in detail his own process of inner transformation under the guidance of his Guru, Bhagavān Nityānanda.

FROM THE FINITE TO THE INFINITE

As Swāmī Muktānanda traveled the world, seekers from many countries asked question after question about their spiritual practices. With profound insight and compassionate humor, Bābā answered them. This volume contains a wealth of those interchanges, offering readers an opportunity to recognize their own questions and to contemplate Bābā's responses.

WHERE ARE YOU GOING?

A lively and anecdotal introduction to the teachings of the Siddha Yoga path, drawn from talks given by Swāmī Muktānanda in public programs in many different times and places. Seasoned practitioners of Siddha Yoga, revisiting this text, will hone their understanding of the path.

BHAGAWAN NITYANANDA OF GANESHPURI

A record of the life and teachings of the Siddha Guru, Bhagavān Nityānanda, written by Swāmī Muktānanda, his foremost disciple and successor. Bhagavān Nityānanda's essential teaching is "The heart is the hub of all sacred places; go there and roam."

ABOUT GURUMAYI CHIDVILĀSĀNANDA

Gurumayi Chidvilāsānanda is the spiritual head of the Siddha Yoga path. She is a Siddha Guru, a meditation Master who has the rare power to awaken within a human being the inner spiritual energy known as *kuṇḍalinī śakti*. In the Siddha Yoga tradition, this sacred initiation is called *śaktipāt dīkṣā*. Thousands of seekers — from a wide range of occupations, nationalities, and cultural backgrounds — have received this initiation from Gurumayi and, with her guidance, progress on their journey to the highest spiritual attainment, the ultimate goal of the Siddha Yoga path.

Born in the south Indian state of Karṇātaka, Gurumayi was still a young child when her family moved to Mumbai. Soon after this, when she was five years old, she visited Gurudev Siddha Peeṭh, the *āśram* of her Guru, Swāmī Muktānanda (known by his students as Bābā). Several times during the first year of her visits, Bābā arranged for Gurumayi to go with a devotee to the nearby village of Gaṇeśpurī for the *darśan* of his own Guru, Bhagavān Nityānanda, who was then in the final months of his life. Throughout her childhood and teenage years, Gurumayi spent many of her weekends and holidays in the serenity and natural beauty of Bābā's *āśram.* Her intense longing to know God fueled her one-pointed focus on meditation, chanting, and *sevā,* selfless service.

During her school vacations, Gurumayi would on occasion travel with Bābā throughout India as he held *satsaṅgs* and taught meditation. In 1970, Bābā began the first of his three world tours, bringing what he called a "meditation revolution" to the West. Gurumayi accompanied Bābā on his second and third tours, and when she was nineteen, she became his English translator at his daily public lectures and meetings with seekers.

As the years passed, in addition to her *sevā* of translating Bābā's spoken word, Gurumayi maintained a disciplined schedule of meditation, chanting, and study of the Indian scriptures; she gave numerous talks about Siddha Yoga philosophy and practices, assisted Bābā with his correspondence, and helped translate his books into English.

In May 1982, Gurumayi was initiated into the ancient Sarasvatī order of monks. Soon after this initiation, in an elaborate and scripturally prescribed ceremony, Bābā installed Gurumayi as a Siddha Yoga Guru and established her as spiritual head of the Siddha Yoga path. Since 1982, Gurumayi, as the Guru, has been imparting the wisdom of her lineage. She has given, and continues to give, *śaktipāt dīkṣā* to seekers from every part of the globe. With compassion she guides Siddha Yoga students of all ages as they put forth disciplined effort on the path. Gurumayi teaches Siddha Yoga meditation and chanting; she writes books of spiritual discourses and poetry, which have been translated into more than twelve languages; she composes and records sacred chants and creates books and music for children; and each year she gives students a unique focus of contemplative study. Through all her words and actions Gurumayi teaches the true meaning of service.

Gurumayi's teachings are also expressed through philanthropic endeavors. In 1992, she inaugurated the PRASAD project, an international not-for-profit organization that provides health, education, and sustainable development programs for children, families, and communities in need. Among PRASAD's many projects are a mobile hospital in rural India, a milk program for school children in the Tansa Valley near Gurudev Siddha Peeṭh, and dental clinics in India and the United States. PRASAD also sponsors eye camps in India and Mexico, which restore sight to thousands of people through free cataract surgery.

The Muktabodha Indological Research Institute, an organization dedicated to preserving and disseminating the scriptures and ancient Vedic traditions of India, is another of Gurumayi's initiatives. Recognizing that the scriptures of India and the oral tradition of the Vedas were being lost in the modern world, Gurumayi created this Institute to preserve and publish important Sanskrit texts, and to develop a *vedaśālā,* a traditional school of Vedic studies, in India.

Whatever form her teachings may take — retreats that focus on meditation and prolonged periods of silence; chanting of scriptures and devotional hymns; philanthropic initiatives; an impromptu gathering with seekers; a word to a student; an extended talk such as those published in her books — Gurumayi is always expressing the same high purpose. She encourages seekers to make the best use of their lives, to discover the divinity at the center of their own being, and to let the joy of this discovery permeate their world.

In her Siddha Yoga Message for the year 2003, Gurumayi describes the essence of her vision for all human beings:

> *In truth, the gift of life must always be recognized and never be taken for granted. Why is life so precious? In Siddha Yoga philosophy, we recognize that in this human life we have a rare opportunity. We can transform an ordinary perception of this universe into an extraordinary vision. To be on this planet and to behold the universe from the divine perspective is a sign of an illumined heart. To put this vision to best use in the best way possible is a human being's highest duty.*

Gurumayi's Guru, Swāmī Muktānanda

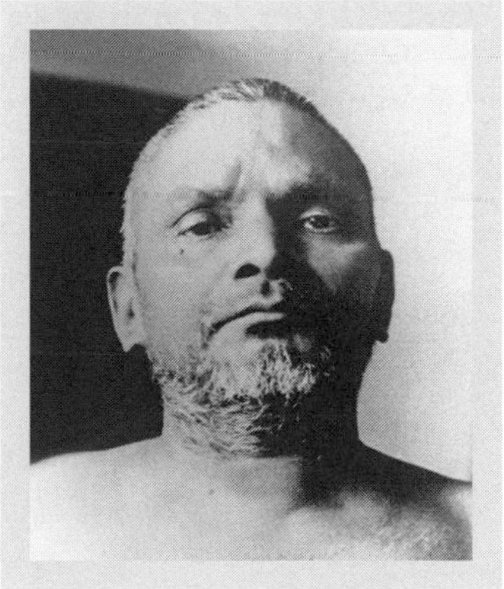

Swāmī Muktānanda's Guru,
Bhagavān Nityānanda

To learn more about
the Siddha Yoga teachings and practices,
visit the Siddha Yoga website at:

www.siddhayoga.org

For further information about
SYDA Foundation books
and audio, video, and DVD recordings,
visit the Siddha Yoga Bookstore website at:

www.siddhayogabookstore.org

or call 845-434-2000 extension 1700.

From the United States and Canada,
call toll-free 888-422-3334.